GREEK SCULPTURE

GREEK SCULPTURE

TEXT AND NOTES BY REINHARD LULLIES

PHOTOGRAPHS BY MAX HIRMER

256 MONOCHROME PLATES

8 COLOR PLATES

HARRY N. ABRAMS, INC., NEW YORK

TRANSLATED FROM THE GERMAN BY
MICHAEL BULLOCK

Nearly all the plates are reproductions from photographs specially taken for this book in the Museums of Greece, as well as those of London, Paris, Rome, Vatican City, Venice and Munich, by the undersigned in collaboration with Miss Julia Asen.

My sincere thanks are due to the Directors and Departmental Heads of the Museums for permitting me to photograph the sculptures and for the support and assistance they so willingly gave me. They are: in Greece, Prof. Christos Karusos, National Museum, Athens; Dr. Jannis Miliadis, Acropolis Museum and Ceramicus Museum, Athens; Dr. Joannes Papadimitriu, Piraeus Museum; Dr. Joanna Konstantinu, Museums in Delphi and Chalcis; Dr. Nikolaos Saphiropulos, Museum in Olympia; Dr. J. P. Kondis, Rhodes; and Dr. M. N. Nikolaidis, Museum in Cos. Also Prof. Bernard Ashmole, British Museum, London; Dr. Jean Charbonneaux, Musée Nationale du Louvre, Paris; Prof. Renato Bartoccini, Museo Nazionale Romano, Rome; Prof. Philippo Magi, Musei Vaticanici, Vatican City; Dr. Bruna Forlati Tamaro, Museo Archeologico, Venice; Prof. H. Diepolder, Staatliche Antikensammlungen, Munich. I wish to extend my particular thanks to Prof. Marinatos of the Ministry of Public Worship and Education in Athens and to the Director of the German Archaeological Institute in Athens, Prof. E. Kunze, for their ready cooperation.

I am indebted to the Heads of the Museum of Fine Arts in Boston and of the Metropolitan Museum of Art in New York for the loan of important Museum photographs; likewise, to Prof. Carl Blümel of the State Museums in Berlin.

My grateful thanks are due also to Dr. Reinhard Lullies, who wrote the text for this book, for his useful advice in the choice of works of art for photographing.

Finally, I take this opportunity to thank Miss Julia Asen for her ever keen collaboration. To her I owe the success of what often proved to be tricky photographs, as well as the careful laying out of the picture material.

Max Hirmer

Our link with Classical Greece is so close that whatever we write on the subject tends to assume the form of a personal declaration of faith. Our response to Greek art – and, in particular, to Greek sculpture – is, if anything, even greater than our response to the epics of Homer ,the Attic tragedies or the philosophy of Plato. For Greek sculpture is the visible and, one might say, the living testimony to the greatness of Greece. It would, however, remain a closed book without scholarly historical research, like everything belonging to the past. Yet the meaning of Greek sculpture far transcends its importance as an historical document. The truth of this – which the Renaissance later adopted as its guiding star – was first recognized during Late Antiquity. The art which the ancient Romans admired and which had a vital formative influence on the artists of Europe from the 15th century onwards, was to become the sole subject worthy of study for Winckelmannn and his contemporaries and, in more recent times, to inspire poets of the stature of Rilke. This powerful influence is due above all to the profound humanity of the Greeks, which is nowhere more manifest than in the dominant place held in Greek sculpture by the human figure. Outlasting two thousand years, these works of art have remained a life-giving source for Western art, and beyond that, a generally accepted measure of human values. Whoever approaches Greek sculpture, be he a layman or a scholar, be he in search of enjoyment or of historical facts, will become aware of its decisive influence, but he must consider at the same time the far-reaching importance of the image of man it has created.

The foundation of the Greek style of sculpture was probably laid by the peoples who came in the Doric migration, about 1200 B.C., from the North to the Greek peninsula and to the coast of Asia Minor, mixing there with the earlier settlers and initiating Greek culture in the true sense of the word. Before this, the art of monumental sculpture had been highly developed in Egypt as well as in the Near East. While we today admire the statues and reliefs by the artists belonging to these older civilizations, we realize that with Greek sculpture a new chapter in the history of world art began. There is an essential contrast between the sculpture of Egypt and the Near East on the one hand and that of Greece on the other. To reduce this to a simple formula: the Egyptians made symbols of reality, but the Greeks created living beings out of stone. In depicting abstractions meant to last into eternity, the Egyptians evolved an immutable artistic language. They reduced the human figure to geometrical shapes meant to be viewed from the front or in profile only and did not suggest a relation of any kind between their statues and the surrounding world. The Greek approach was essentially different, in that the artist sought to create a perfect and living organism, to infuse his statue down to the finger-tips with the breath of life and to endow it with a natural relationship to space. Any work of Greek art,

It was above all Athens which, at the peak of its political power after the Persian War, attracted artists from abroad and became a focal point at which they were fused together. The genius of the Athenian Phidias outshone all other sculptors. His fame in the ancient world was based particularly on the two colossal religious images of gold and ivory, Athena Parthenos and Zeus, at Olympia, which perished in late antiquity and of which we can only form an idea from descriptions and copies. Other images of the gods, statues of Hermes, Apollo and Athene, and also a wounded Amazon in bronze, have survived in Roman marble copies. Apart from these statues, we can – by a rare and fortunate chance of survival – see Phidias's 5th-century originals in the Parthenon sculptures. In the metopes, the frieze and the pediments of the Parthenon he reached *140–169* the pinnacle of his personal achievement, and at the same time Greek sculpture entered its Classical stage. As the blossom develops from the bud overnight, so this stage was attained in the Parthenon sculptures without any transition, even in relation to what immediately preceded it. Everything about them is entirely original, brilliant and magnificent – the mastery of formal and compositional problems as well as the rendering of the mythological material and the heightened ethos of the figures. In the southern metopes the Centaurs are no longer the rough, *140–145* brutish fellows we see being slaughtered by the Lapithae in the west pediment of the Temple of Zeus at Olympia. Here they oppose the Lapithae almost on equal terms, and are not only vanquished but also victors. Battle as such is presented in the Parthenon metopes in a fresh, exalted and refined light. A new feature within the framework of the Doric temple is the frieze high up *146–161* on the exterior of the cella. Also without precedent and without any real successor is the theme of the procession received by the gods. The vast mythological visions on the pediments are no less unique: in the east, the miraculous birth of Athene in the presence of the great Olympian *162–167* deities, on a day which Helios brings up with his quadriga on one side, while on the other Selene goes down with her steeds into the waters of Ocean; in the west, Athene's struggle with Posei- *168, 169* don for the Attic land in the presence of the gods and heroes from the Athenian citadel.

It would be a mistake to imagine that the harmony of Classical art corresponded to a tranquil outer existence or a period of peace and prosperity in 5th-century Greece. Behind the order and moderation of Classical art was a knowledge of the potentialities and limits of human nature, a clear perception that sprang from concentrated intellectual analysis of the conflict between the wishes of the individual and the demands made upon him by Religion and the State – those supra-personal powers which then enjoyed unquestioned acceptance and provided everyone with a secure framework for his own existence. Unity of form and content, the essence of Classical art, mirrors a certain idea of man which, for the Greeks at that juncture in world history, was an absolutely obligatory aim and ideal.

The equipoise of forces, as given universal expression in Polyclitus's canon and the Parthenon, was limited to a short span of time. It is true that the Peloponnesian War (431–404 B.C.), at the end of which the hegemony of Athens in Greece was broken, did not initially cause any break in artistic evolution; but already in the generation following the Parthenon, works like the bronze statuette of a girl from Beroea, the boy in the Piraeus Museum or the tombstone *194; 190* of Dexileos foreshadow new trends that are evident in the altered balance of the individual *191* figure as well as in the changed relationship between the figures and the background in relief sculpture.

Fourth-century figures are no longer self-contained in the same way as the Polyclitus bronze in the Louvre. As the result of a greater differentiation between supporting and free leg and a consequent increase in the shift of the axes of the body, these figures swing farther towards one side or the other, the centre of gravity is displaced from the middle and not infrequently a support is included in the composition, as is the case with the girl from Beroea and, at a later stage, the Hermes of Praxiteles. In the same degree to which they have abandoned their secure stance and inner firmness, they have, as it were, grown into surrounding space, which in the early 4th century begins to encircle and play around them as atmosphere and gradually appears in more and more distinct contrast to them.

With the figures' increasing mobility and more profound spatial evolution, the image of the human being becomes richer and more differentiated. Thus woman is rendered in all her specific femininity, as in the rare perfection of the beautiful head from Tegea, the Demeter from Cnidus, or the delicate head of a girl from Chios. The little Dionysus on the arm of the Hermes at Olympia, and the weeping boy crouching beside the hunter in the picture on the Ilissus stele, are portrayed as real children with childish forms and ways. Further, the relation between mother and daughter, father and son, husband and wife, as well as the various ages of man, are more finely distinguished. This is easily seen from the series of Attic sepulchral reliefs reproduced here. In general, the portrayal of mental processes through expression, pose and gesture gains ever-increasing importance in the course of the 4th century B.C. According to ancient tradition, Praxiteles was a pioneer in this direction, and we find this confirmed by his surviving work as well as by sculpture produced under his influence. With the progressive differentiation of the human image, the treatment of the individual portrait also underwent a change from a more or less supra-personal reproduction of outward appearance at the beginning of the 4th century B.C., which was still rooted in the high Classicism of the Parthenon period, to a more individual – one might go so far as to say more naturalistic – conception of the portrait at the end of the same century. The bronze head of an African from Cyrene, the magnificent statue of the supposed Mausolus and the boxer from Olympia, shown here, are both important and typical examples of Greek sculpture at this period.

The stylistic differences between the various provinces of art, some of which may be traced as far as the end of the 5th century B.C., become less numerous during the 4th century. In the Greek motherland those two provinces assume leadership in the field of sculpture in which the Classical form attained its maximum development: Attica, and the north-east Peloponnesus. Several names of artists and works of art from the school of Polyclitus, who was probably rather younger than Phidias, have come down to us through literature. The Polyclitan tradition is still perceptible during the second half of the 4th century B.C. in such works as the bronze youth from Anticythera or the relief from the base of a column in the later Artemision at Ephesus. The most famous master of Sicyonian metal-casting was Lysippus, whose extremely fertile working life must have extended over more than six decades and lasted until towards the

199; 216, 217
228, 229
220–223; 218

198
205–207;
224, 225

208, 209, 213
214, 215

22

end of the 4th century B.C. Of similar importance and influence in Athens were Praxiteles, who worked chiefly in marble, and Leochares, who collaborated with Lysippus during the Alexandrian period. It is typical of the times that one of the greatest monuments of the 4th century was not publicly commissioned, but erected on the orders of a single ruling personage. This was the colossal tomb of Mausolus at Halicarnassus, the sculptural decoration on which brought together in the residence of the Lesser Asian prince four of the most celebrated Greek sculptors *201–204* of the day – Scopas, Timotheus, Bryaxis and Leochares.

Again, it is instructive to trace the changes of form that took place during the 4th century B.C. in the relief style also. Two Attic sepulchral reliefs portraying a similar scene afford an illuminating comparison: the tombstone of Hegeso dating from the end of the 5th century, and a *185* tombstone three or four decades later in date showing a woman and her maidservant, both of *196, 197* which are in the National Museum, Athens. In Hegeso's tombstone the inner link between the two figures is expressed through the slight inclination of the heads, the use made of the box which the maidservant is holding out to the seated woman and from which the latter has taken the jewellery, the position of the arms and the close contiguity of the hands, the framing outlines of the curved chair and the long robe falling at the maidservant's back. In the superficially similar 4th-century relief, the serving-girl stands on her own with the box in her hand; she holds it close to her, raises the lid and looks down at it. The bowed, seated mistress and the striding maidservant are so firmly enveloped in their garments that every movement of the limbs and every curve of the body comes up against the resistance of the fabric. There is no longer anything connective about the straight lines of the seat. The figures have become more independent and possess a deeper spatial volume, they stand out from the background with well-defined contours and the background itself acquires greater solidity and autonomy in relation to the figures.

As the 4th century progresses, the figures approach more and more closely to free sculpture, as may be seen in the sepulchral stele from the Ilissus, the tombstone from Rhamnus or the late *218, 219* fragment with the bearded man in a cloak. They gradually lose their connexion with the back- *226, 227* ground and become isolated from it, while the background increasingly asserts its own independence and finally assumes the character of a wall that stands in marked contrast to the figures. In the end, the two elements whose active interrelationship gave life to the Greek relief of the 5th and 4th centuries, lose almost all connexion with one another. Thus it may be said that when Demetrius of Phaleron's proscription of luxury brought the carving of Attic sepulchral reliefs to an end in the last phases of the 4th century, this end had already been adumbrated by the artistic evolution of this form of sculpture.

Roughly a hundred years separate Hegeso's tombstone from the fragment of a late Attic *185* sepulchral relief showing a bearded man in a cloak just referred to. This century was also a time *226, 227* of revolutionary changes. At its beginning the Greek city-states were still fighting for hegemony in Greece, during the Peloponnesian War, as closed political units; at its end, the individual communities had lost their independence and freedom in the struggles against Philip of Macedon and Alexander. Alexander had carried Greek culture as far as India. After his premature death

(323 B.C.) Alexander's empire fell to his successors. The Greek motherland was thereafter forced to relinquish its pre-eminent role in the political and artistic domains to the courts of the Diadochi. Among the latter, the kings of Alexandria, Syria, Pergamon and Bithynia, in particular, gathered poets, scholars and sculptors around them during the 3rd and 2nd centuries B.C. and commissioned work from them.

By the end of the 4th century B.C., tendencies were becoming noticeable in sculpture that can only be regarded as a reaction against preceding epochs. They did not bear full fruit until the 3rd century, the first century of Hellenistic sculpture, generally described as the period of the "simple style" and "closed form". The great sweeping movement that still passes through each *219; 220–223* of the figures on the sepulchral relief from Rhamnus and the Hermes of Praxiteles began to grow rigid during the last quarter of the 4th century. Instead of the clear arrangement of axes which had determined the construction of figures for so long, overlapping of the parts and opposing rhythms now became essential elements of sculpture. The inner structure of the figures became firmer, even stiff, and also more complicated. They no longer reach out into space, as they had done before, but stand in opposition to their surroundings, becoming concentrated – by means of carefully thought-out poses and movements – about a newly created centre. It is no coincidence that, after the early Hellenistic period, draped statues acquire increased importance, alongside statues of naked athletes and images of unclothed Aphrodite. Drapery is now set free from the body and employed as an independent element in the composition, in which it is required to fulfil a definite structural function, serving either to support the body or to enclose *231* it, as in the statue of the priestess Nikokleia from Cnidus, which was carved soon after the middle of the 3rd century B.C. Here the forms of the body vanish behind the vertical folds of the finely puckered chiton, which looks like a curtain, and behind the cloak on top of it, whose thick material and folds running diagonally across the body are in marked contrast to the long undergarment. It is interesting to cast a glance back from this tightly self-contained statue, *200* isolated from everything outside itself, to the Demeter at Venice, with its relatively broad and clear structure and stance, its comparatively simple arrangement of the peplos and cloak, in order to see the distance travelled by the development of the standing female draped statue from the mid-4th to the mid-3rd century B.C.

232, 233 The sacrificial servant in the Museo delle Terme, which comes from a Roman villa near Antium, is also very typical of the style that characterized the third quarter of the 3rd century B.C. With perfect mastery of his medium, the artist has recorded in this exceedingly charming work a fleeting situation. The girl, portrayed in the act of walking, is entirely absorbed by her task: she is taking a sacrificial implement or an offering from the round salver she holds in her left hand. All the main lines of the composition lead to this centre. In spite of the opposing directions of the movements and the overlapping limbs, garments and folds, this statue, too, gives the impression of being firmly shut off from everything outside it. The statue is clearly intended to be seen from one particular angle. Its artistic qualities are most manifest when it is looked at diagonally from its right side. The Hellenistic bronze original from which this statue of the sacrificial servant is derived must itself have stood in front of a wall or in a niche, a

24

position in which free sculpture was frequently placed during the 3rd century B.C., as we know from literary sources. Thus an extract from the writings of Callixeinus of Rhodes quoted by Athenaeus (196a and ff.) tells us that a hundred marble figures by leading masters stood in front of the rectangular stanchion of the pavilion erected for Ptolemy II at Alexandria in ca. 270 B.C. And three statues of members of the Alexandrian ruling house were placed between Ionic columns in front of the wall of an Early Hellenistic nymphaeum described in a poem dating from the first half of the 3rd century B.C. The placing of statues in this position is an expression of a particular feeling for space current at that time, and also manifest in the style of 3rd-century reliefs. If a marked isolation of the figures both from one another and from the background is already evident in 4th-century reliefs, the 3rd century goes still farther in this direction. It is characteristic of the intrinsic structure of Early Hellenistic reliefs, for example, that the individual figures lean against a tree, a pillar or a column, objects which operate in the composition like a piece of scenery and evoke the impression of a solid boundary or of several distinct layers of space.

In the Lesser Asian votive relief to Cybele and Attis at Venice, which belongs to the same *230* period as the Nikokleia and the Antium Girl, each of the two main figures is portrayed on its own and at a marked interval from the other. The deities stand in statuesque pose and dimensions in front of the wall of their shrine, which is broken by a lofty door with a half-open and foreshortened right leaf, through which the woman worshipper has entered the sacred precincts with a little serving maid. The figures and the background are here assigned to two different and contrasting spheres of art. This antithesis between the elements of the relief probably explains why the 3rd century B.C., compared with the Classical epoch, showed little taste for relief sculpture. By nature it was a period of statuesque free sculpture. The preconditions for the relief style of the succeeding period rested on a new relationship between the figure and the surface.

This mutation in the history of Hellenistic sculpture, however, means nothing else than the dissolution of "closed form". It must have taken place at the end of the 3rd and the beginning of the 2nd centuries. In our selection, two masterpieces of the highest quality convincingly demonstrate the transition from the "closed form" and the "simple style" of the 3rd, to the "open form" and "pathetic style" of the 2nd century: the Sleeping Satyr from the Barberini *234, 235* Collection in the Munich Glyptothek and the Nike donated by the Rhodians to Samothrace *248* as a votive offering in gratitude for their victories over Antiochus III of Syria around 190 B.C. The outline of the mighty, outstretched sleeper, sunk in oppressive dreams, originally – as restored in modern times the left arm and right leg do not occupy quite their old position – fitted into a wide parallelogram. The practice of focusing the composition on a centre, which was characteristic of mid-3rd century sculpture, has been abandoned by the artist of the later 3rd century in this magnificent figure. The sculptural form as such has also changed in comparison with older works. It has become looser, the surface transitions are more lively. Light and shade play a greater part in the modelling than hitherto. The Victory of Samothrace goes considerably farther than the Munich Satyr in its use of the plane, although the Nike now seems

25

9 Reclining lion, head, cf. Plate 8. Corfu

10   Head of Hera. From the Heraion at Olympia. Limestone. Olympia

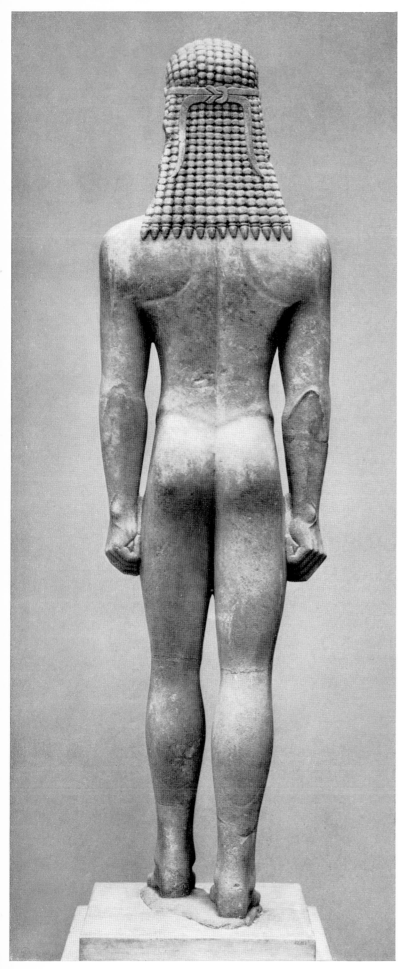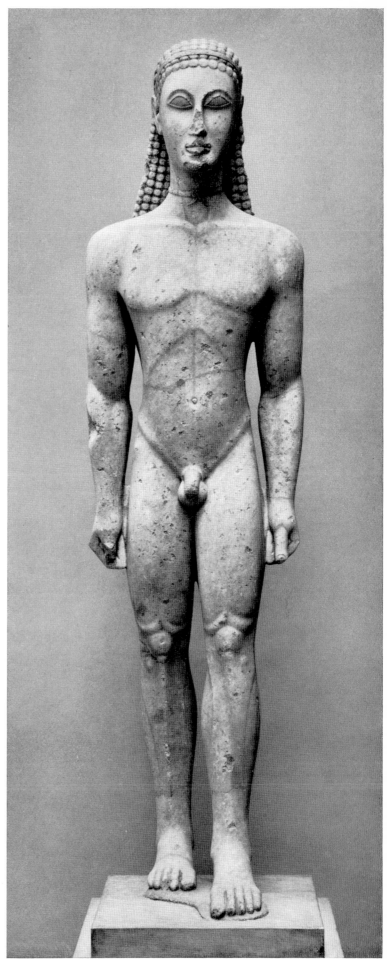

11 Standing youth, found in Attica. Marble. New York

12   Standing youth, head, cf. Plate 11. New York

13 Standing youth, head, cf. Plate 11. New York

25 Sculptures from the pediment of the Hekatompedon on the Athenian Acropolis. Limestone. Acropolis Museum, Athens
top: Right half of the pediment with the three-bodied monster   bottom: Forepart of the three-bodied monster

26 Youth from the sanctuary of the Ptoan Apollo in Boeotia. Front view of head. Limestone
National Museum, Athens

27   Youth from the sanctuary of the Ptoan Apollo in Boeotia. Side view of head. Limestone.
National Museum, Athens

28   Rider, found on the Athenian Acropolis. Marble from Paros. Acropolis Museum, Athens, and Paris

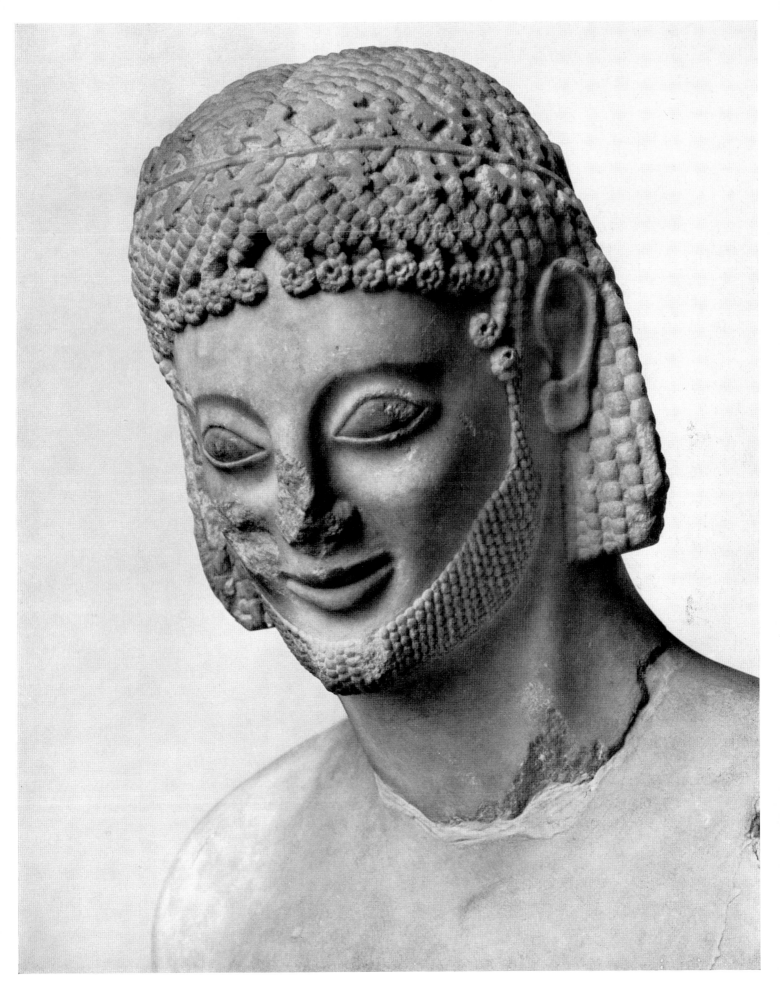

29 Rider's head (so-called Rampin head). Marble from Paros. Paris

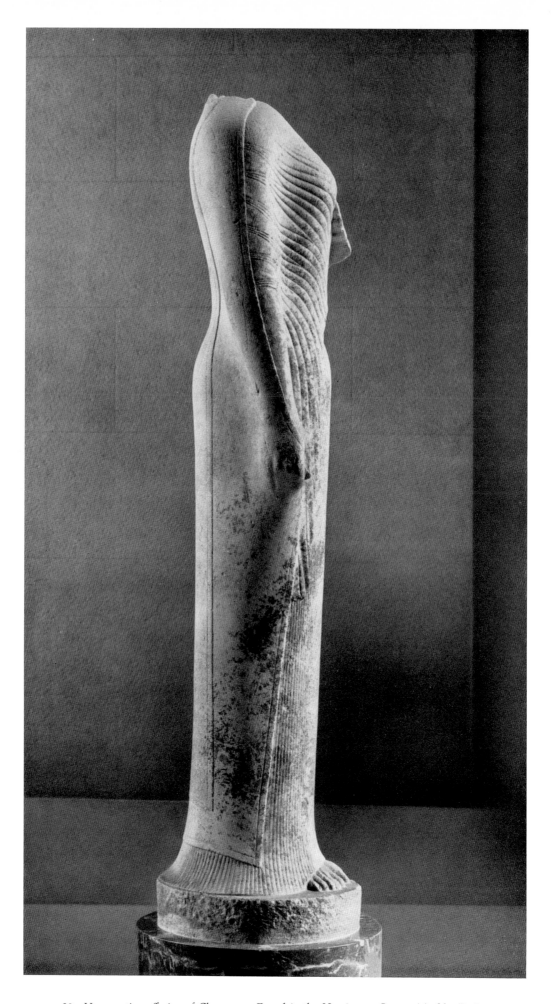

30 Hera, votive offering of Cheramyes. Found in the Heraion on Samos. Marble. Paris

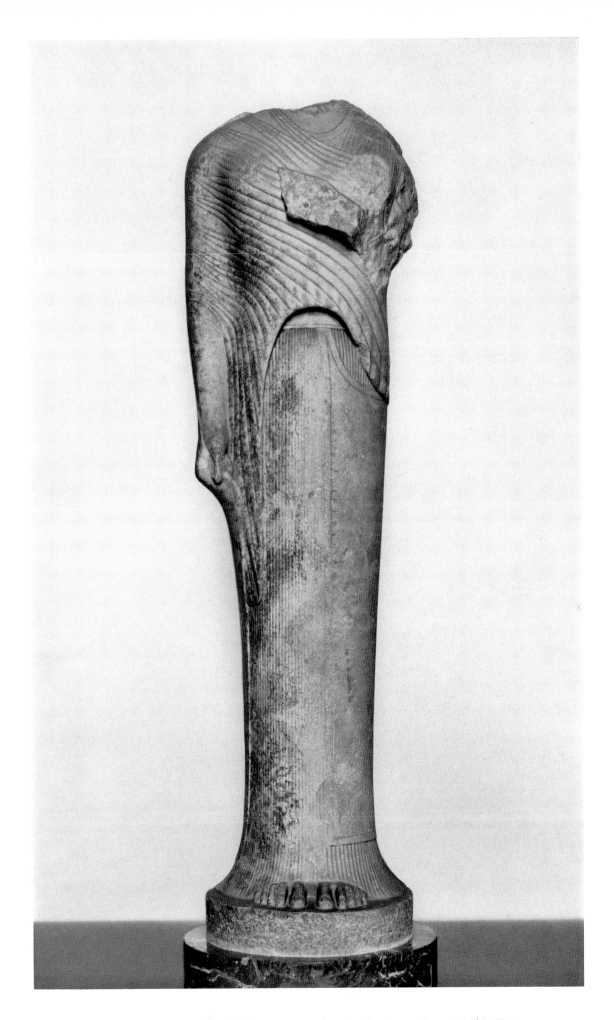

31 Hera, votive offering of Cheramyes. Found in the Heraion on Samos. Marble. Paris

32 Standing youth from Melos. Marble from Naxos. National Museum, Athens

33 Standing youth from Melos, head. Marble from Naxos. National Museum, Athens

34   Standing youth (so-called Apollo of Tenea), found at Tenea, near Corinth. Marble from Paros. Munich

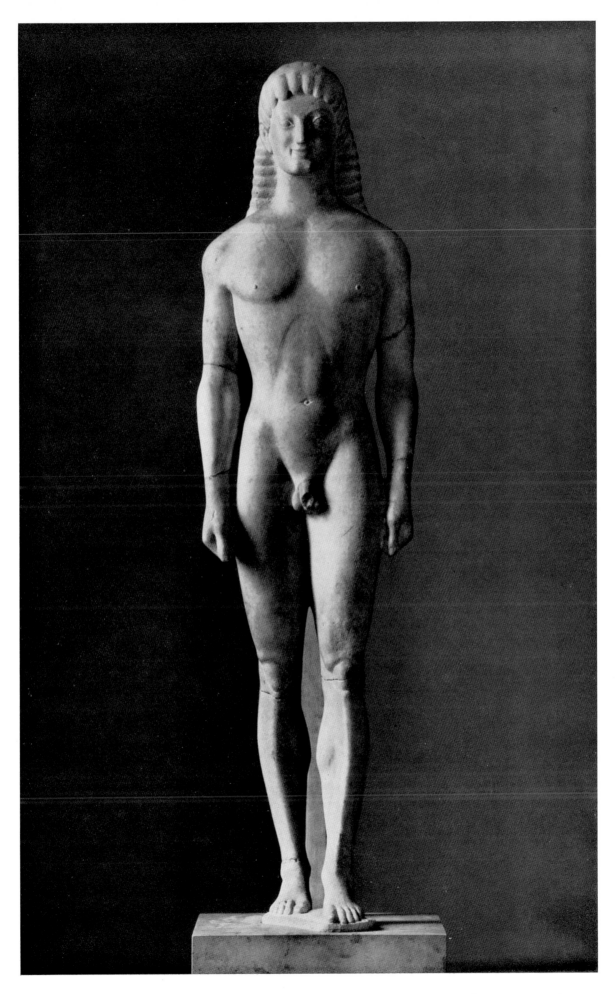

35   Standing youth (so-called Apollo of Tenea), found at Tenea, near Corinth. Marble from Paros. Munich

36 Standing youth (so-called Apollo of Tenea), found at Tenea, near Corinth. Marble from Paros. Munich

37   From the sepulchral stele of a discus-bearer. Found at Athens. Marble from Paros. National Museum, Athens

38 Head found at Ephesus. Marble. London

39 Head found at Ephesus. Marble. London

40 Female figure. Fragment of relief from the base of a pillar in the old Temple of Apollo at Didyma, near Miletus
Marble from Korossai. Berlin

41 Standing girl (kore) in chiton and peplos. Marble from Paros. Acropolis Museum, Athens

42 Head of the standing girl in chiton and peplos. Marble from Paros. National Museum, Athens

43 Head of the standing girl in chiton and peplos. Marble from Paros. National Museum, Athens

59 Detail from the base of a statue found at Athens. Spear-thrower from the relief in Plate 58 top

60 Detail from the base of a statue found at Athens. Young people with dog and cat, left half of relief

61 Detail from the base of a statue found at Athens. Young people with dog and cat, right half of relief

62 Sculpture from the west pediment of the Temple of Apollo Daphnophoros at Eretria on Euboea.
Theseus and Antiopeia. Marble from Paros. Chalkis

63   Sculpture from the west pediment of the Temple of Apollo Daphnophoros at Eretria on Euboea.
Theseus and Antiopeia. Marble from Paros. Chalkis

77 Girl in chiton and cloak, head. Acropolis Museum, Athens

78 From the east pediment of the so-called Temple of Aphaia on Aegina: Head of Pallas Athene.
Marble from Paros. Munich

79 From the east pediment of the so-called Temple of Aphaia on Aegina: Hurrying rescuer.
Marble from Paros. Munich

80   From the east pediment of the so-called Temple of Aphaia on Aegina: Dying warrior.
Marble from Paros. Munich

81 Dying warrior, cf. Plate 80

93   Enthroned goddess, from Taranto. Marble from Paros. Berlin

94 Enthroned goddess, from Taranto. Marble from Paros. Berlin

95   Enthroned goddess, from Taranto. Marble from Paros. Berlin

96   Enthroned goddess, from Taranto, head. Berlin

97 Enthroned goddes, from Taranto, head in profile. Berlin

98 Charioteer, votive offering of Polyzalos of Gela for Delphi. Bronze. Delphi

107   Athene, from the metope in Plate 106

108 From the east pediment of the Temple of Zeus at Olympia: Central group: Zeus between Oinomaos (right) and Pelops (left).
Marble from Paros. Olympia

109   From the east pediment of the Temple of Zeus at Olympia: Right-hand continuation of the central group:
Sterope (left), kneeling girl and horses from the quadriga of Pelops (right). Marble from Paros. Olympia

110 From the east pediment of the Temple of Zeus at Olympia: Myrtilos, Oinamaos's charioteer.
Marble from Paros. Olympia

111   From the east pediment of the Temple of Zeus at Olympia: Crouching youth, from the northern
half of the pediment. Marble from Paros. Olympia

112 From the east pediment of the Temple of Zeus at Olympia: The seer, from the northern half of the pediment. Marble from Paros. Olympia

113   Head of the seer, cf. Plate 112

114 From the east pediment of the Temple of Zeus at Olympia: Groom, so-called Kladeos, from the northern corner of the pediment. Marble from Paros. Olympia

115 From the west pediment of the Temple of Zeus at Olympia: Lapithan woman, from the northern corner of the pediment. Marble from Paros. Olympia

116   From the west pediment of the Temple of Zeus at Olympia: The two three-figure groups:
a Lapithan man and woman fighting a centaur. Marble from Paros. Olympia

117 From the west pediment of the Temple of Zeus at Olympia: The Lapithan woman from the upper three-figure group shown in Plate 116

118 From the west pediment of the Temple of Zeus at Olympia: The bride of the Lapithan King Peirithoos, attacked by a centaur. Marble from Paros. Olympia

119 Peirithoos's bride, cf. Plate 118

120 Apollo, cf. Plate 121

121 From the west pediment of the Temple of Zeus at Olympia: Apollo. Marble from Paros. Olympia

122   From the west pediment of the Temple of Zeus at Olympia: Two-figure group from the southern half of the
pediment: Lapithan and biting centaur. Marble from Paros. Olympia

133 Head of Aphrodite, cf. Plate 132

134 From the so-called Ludovisian Throne: Side panel with female flute-player. Marble from Paros.
National Museum, Rome

135 From the so-called Ludovisian Throne: Side panel with young woman taking incense from a box.
Marble from Paros. National Museum, Rome

136   Votive relief tondo, from Melos. Marble from Paros. National Museum, Athens

137   Votive relief to Athene. Marble. Acropolis Museum, Athens

145   Centaur and Lapithan, from the metope in Plate 143

146 From the Parthenon on the Athenian Acropolis. Frieze on the western face of the cella seen from below. Acropolis, Athens

147 From the Parthenon on the Athenian Acropolis. Equestrian group from the west frieze. Marble from Mount Pentelicus. London

148 From the Parthenon on the Athenian Acropolis. Above: Equestrian groups from the south frieze
Centre and bottom: Equestrian groups from the north frieze. Marble from Mount Pentelicus. London

149 From the Parthenon on the Athenian Acropolis.
Equestrian group from the north frieze, cf. Plate 148 centre, left-hand panel. London

150   From the Parthenon on the Athenian Acropolis. Equestrian group from the north frieze, cf. Plate 184 centre, right-hand panel. London

151   From the Parthenon on the Athenian Acropolis. Equestrian group from the north frieze, cf. Plate 148 centre, centre panel. London

152 From the Parthenon on the Athenian Acropolis. From the north frieze. Acropolis Museum, Athens

153 From the Parthenon on the Athenian Acropolis. From the south frieze: Festival organizer and sacrificial bull. London

169 From the Parthenon on the Athenian Acropolis.
From the west pediment: Iris (left) and Amphitrite (right). Marble from Mount Pentelicus. London

170 Votive relief to the Eleusinian deities: Dispatch of Triptolemos. Marble from Mount Pentelicus. National Museum, Athens

171   Triptolemos receiving the ears of corn from the hand of Demeter, cf. Plate 170

172 Dying Niobid. Marble from Paros. National Museum, Rome

173   Dying Niobid. Marble from Paros. National Museum, Rome

183 Funerary relief with Timarista and Krito. Marble. Rhodes

184   Fragment of a sepulchral stele, from Athens. Marble from Mount Pentelicus. National Museum, Athens

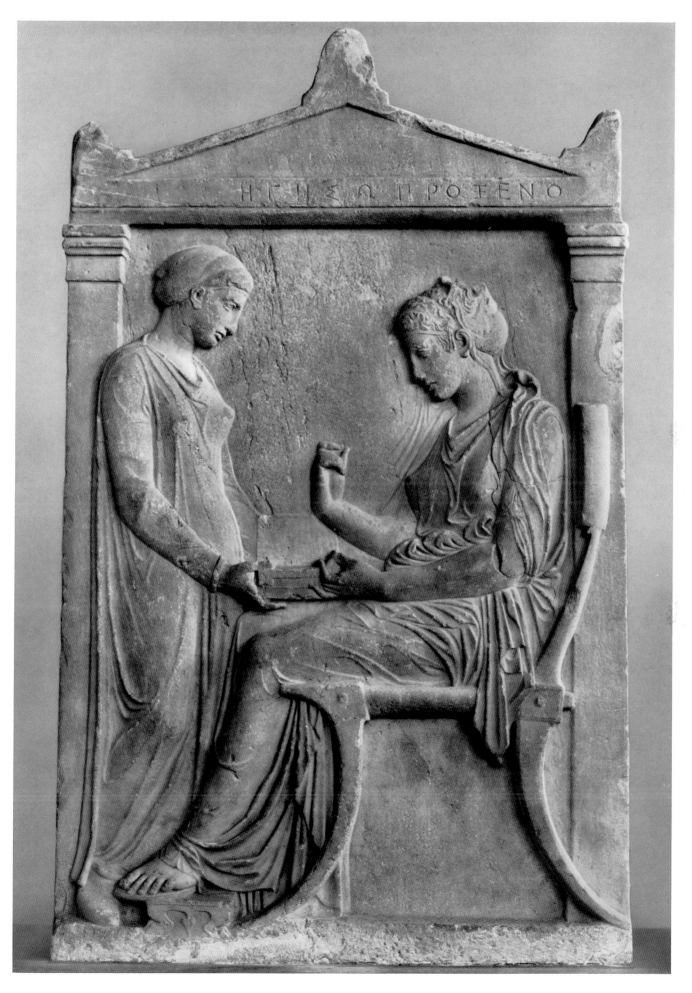

185 Sepulchral monument of Hegeso. Marble from Mount Pentelicus. National Museum, Athens

186 Votive relief from Athens: Abduction of Basile by Echelos. National Museum, Athens
facing:
187 From the balustrade on the temple of Athene Nike on the Athenian Acropolis. Marble from Mount Pentelicus. Acropolis Museum, Athens
Top: Athene and Nike decorating the Tropeion   Bottom: Two winged victories leading a bull to the sacrifice

195 From an Attic funerary urn: Couple bidding one another farewell. Marble from Mount Pentelicus. Munich

196   Sepulchral monument of an unknown woman with her maidservant, from Piraeus.
Marble from Mount Pentelicus. National Museum, Athens

197   From the monument in Plate 196

198   Portrait head of an African, from Cyrene. Bronze. London

199   Head of Hygieia, from Tegea. Marble from Mount Pentelicus. National Museum, Athens

217 Head of Demeter from Cnidus, cf. Plate 216

218　Sepulchral monument of a youth, from the Ilissus at Athens. Marble from Mount Pentelicus. National Museum, Athens

219   Attic sepulchral relief, from Rhamnus in Attica. Marble from Mount Pentelicus. National Museum, Athens

220   Hermes with the Dionysus boy. Marble from Paros. Olympia

221   Hermes with the Dionysus boy. Marble from Paros. Olympia

235 Head of the sleeping satyr in Plate 234

236   Portrait head of a philosopher, found in the sea off Anticythera. Profile. Bronze. National Museum, Athens

237   Portrait head of a philosopher, found in the sea off Anticythera. Bronze. National Museum, Athens

238   Northern projection of the Pergamon altar. Berlin
On the front: Triton and Amphitrite
On the stair side: Nereus and Doris

239 From the Great Frieze of the Pergamon altar. Western face of the northern projection:
Nereus and Doris (left) and antagonist of Doris (right). Marble. Berlin

240 From the Great Frieze of the Pergamon altar. From the east frieze:
Zeus (left) and Porphyrion, the antagonist of Zeus (right). Marble. Berlin

255   Head of the Aphrodite from Melos, cf. Plate 254

256   Aphrodite, terra-cotta statuette. Berlin

257   Crouching Aphrodite, from Rhodes. Marble from Paros. Rhodes

258   Male portrait head, from Delos. Bronze. National Museum, Athens

259   Head of the boxer in Plates 260 and 261

marble from the islands of Korossai (Phurni) near Icaria. Height 22" (55.5 cm.). State Museum, Berlin, Department of Classical Antiquities, No. 1721.

Little has survived of the old Temple of Apollo at Didyma, which was destroyed by the Persians in 494 B.C. It was an Ionian building of very large proportions, with a double arcade of eight columns in front, which – as in the Temple of Artemis at Ephesus (see 214, 215) – stood on high plinths decorated with reliefs and about a yard and a half in diameter. The relief shows a roughly life-size clothed figure seen from the front, as to the name and nature of which we have no reliable evidence. The neck of the dress is modelled and traces of red paint on the right side of the figure just below the throat suggest that a second garment under the first may have been indicated by paint alone. A linen head-dress forms a wide and beautifully curved arc over brow and temples. On top of this lies a thick cord that was no doubt intended to hold the head-cloth in position. A rolled curl hangs down in front of each ear. From beneath them emerge two ribbons that fall down over shoulders and arms, possibly the end of a band of cloth that ran across the forehead – where it was only painted in – and was tied at the back. Further traces of red paint show that the figure was also adorned with a double necklace. The broad, softly rounded face with its serene and impassive expression, reminiscent of the calm, detached look of Asiatic countenances, is very characteristic of the fragment's style. The wide mouth with the narrow, sharply defined lips, and the slit eyes with their heavy lids, look as though they had been scored into the swelling, opulent forms. We must recognize in this fragment the handiwork of an East Ionian artist of the third quarter of the 6th century B.C.

Jb. Wiegand, Didyma. First Part: Die Baubeschreibung in drei Bänden von H. Knackfuß (1941), 123 f. and 196 f., plate 214, fig. F 724. — C. Weickert, Griechische Plastik (1946), 14 ff., fig. 6.

41–43
STANDING GIRL IN CHITON AND PEPLOS. Parian marble. Height including the inch-high-plinth 4' (1.21 m.). Found on the Athenian Acropolis, 1886. Acropolis Museum, Athens, No. 679.

This statue is only distinguished outwardly, by the clothes, from the figures of girls on the Acropolis – the korai – belonging to the same period. The girl is wearing a girded Dorian peplos with an over-fold, and under this a fine linen chiton whose wide selvage is visible at the throat and whose fine, wavy folds appear beneath the peplos. The figure stands stiffly and erect, the feet together, the head looking straight in front and tilted a fraction to the left in conformity with the slightly raised left shoulder. The body is concealed by the heavy woollen material of the peplos but clearly perceptible in the curves and hollows of the modelling. There is something block-like about the lower part of the body, which is flat in front and rounded at the back. The right arm hangs down at the side slightly bent at the elbow, the hand rests against the thigh holding a wreath or sprig. The outstretched left fore-arm was made separately and inserted. The artistic qualities of the work are most clearly manifest in the powerful, rich forms of the head and the festal serenity of the expression of the face. The abundant hair frames the forehead in waves, lies in three curled plaits on each shoulder, and hangs down over the back in broad indented strands held together by a band. A bronze wreath

encircled the hair. The ears were adorned with metal pendants. The statue is the mature work of one of the leading Attic sculptors of the period around 530 B.C. At least two other works have been attributed to the same hand – an equestrian statue from the Acropolis (the head of which is in the Louvre) and a female head from the same site, both of them older and dating from the mid-century.

The ancient painting on this "kore in the peplos" is well preserved. The border of the robe at the throat is green. The lower border of the over-fold bears a green palmette pattern and above this a pattern of green spirals. The ends of the green-striped girdle hanging down at the sides are bound with two wide strips of green braid with brightly coloured rosettes. The hair, lips and iris are red, the pupils, brows and lashes black, the neckband green.

H. Payne and G. M. Young, Archaic Marble Sculpture from the Acropolis, 18 f., plates 29—33; 38, 5. — H. Schrader, Die archaischen Marmorbildwerke der Akropolis, No. 4. plates 3—8. — E. Langlotz and W. H. Schuchhardt, Archaische Plastik auf der Akropolis (1938), 10—13.

44–51
PANELS FROM THE FRIEZES ON THE TREASURE-HOUSE OF THE SIPHNIANS AT DELPHI. Parian marble. Museum, Delphi.

The treasury erected in the sanctuary of Apollo at Delphi by the inhabitants of the island of Siphnos as a votive offering and for the storage of their bequests was built shortly before 525 B.C., as we know from Herodotus III, 57 and Pausanias X, 11, 2. It was constructed throughout of Parian marble, had a ground-plan of 18'8" × 27'7", and stood on a high limestone foundation at the foot of the steep and rugged Phaedriades, below the terrace of the temple, facing west. Its shape was that of a small temple with projecting side walls, decorated on the outside with a tremendous wealth of figurative and ornamental sculpture. Two female figures carried the entablature on the west front; only a few remains have survived from the pediment on this side. The east pediment shows Hercules carrying off the Delphic tripod.

A relief frieze showing mythological scenes ran round the whole building above the architrave, 25.2" to 27.3" (on the west front) high and 87'8" long. It was framed by magnificent sculptured decorative fillets, with Ionic cymas at the top and Lesbian cymas at the bottom. More than half the frieze is still in existence. Stylistically, two masters can be distinguished. One was responsible for the west and south faces showing the Judgement of Paris and the seizure of Leucippides by the Dioscuri, the other for the east and north faces. Practically nothing now remains in situ save the foundations and the marble steps that carried the superstructure. The other remains are housed in the Museum at Delphi.

Plates 44–51 show parts of the east frieze (44 top, 45) with seated deities on either side of a now missing centrepiece and a battle scene, and parts of the north frieze (44 centre and bottom, 46–51) that ran along what was later the Sacred Way, with scenes from the war of the gods against the giants.

In the gathering of gods on the east frieze (44 top, 45), the gods on the side of the Trojans sit on the left – Ares, Aphrodite, Artemis and Apollo, who is turning round to speak to the two goddesses behind him, and Zeus. Facing them on the right are the goddesses siding with the Greeks – Athene, Hera and Hebe.

The character of each one is splendidly brought out and they participate with lively gestures in the events which elicit their passionate interest.

The long panel with the fight over a fallen warrior (44 centre) shows, on the left, the Trojans (from the centre, Hector (?), Aeneas, and Glaucus, looking round, with a quadriga), and on the right, the Greeks (Menelaus with a gorgoneion as a shield emblem, an unknown man, Automedon, looking round and with a quadriga, and Nestor standing at the side with his right arm raised). Some of the figures are identified by inscriptions.

In the north frieze (44 bottom, 46–51) the gods are fighting from left to right against the giants, who are attacking from the other side. The giants are represented as heavily armed, equipped with helmets and shields, and some also with breastplates and greaves. They fight with spears, swords, stones and boulders. At the left-hand extremity of the frieze, in the east, Hephaestus in the short chiton of the craftsman stands at his bellows; in front of him are two unnamed goddesses, perhaps Demeter and Kore. Facing them are some giants. These are followed by Dionysus with the panther skin and Cybele with her chariot drawn by lions, which are attacking a giant; then come Apollo and Artemis, who are shooting bows. The fleeing giant in front of them, who is looking back over his shoulder, wears a *kantharus,* or two-handled drinking vessel, worked into the crest of his helmet; the giant himself is named as Kantharos in an inscription. In front of him is a fallen warrior and three further giants. In the adjoining panel Zeus races forward on a quadriga; in front of him are Hera bending down to a fallen warrior, Athene with the aegis, Ares with helmet and shield over the prostrate body of a dead giant whose head is seen front-face; then comes Hermes with his pointed hat, a skin over his chiton and a broad sword-sheath in his left hand, turning towards onrushing giants; and finally Poseidon and Amphitrite (?), of the lower half of whose bodies only fragments remain on the edge of the panel. The background of the frieze was blue, the foot-fillet red. The hair, the crests of the helmets, the inside of the shields, and the manes and tails of the horses, were also red. Traces of red paint have also been left on some of the garments.

The liveliness and refinement of its execution, and its importance in the history of art, render the frieze on the Siphnian treasure-house a masterpiece of Archaic relief sculpture. The north-east master, a Parian artist, must have been one of the leading sculptors of his day, full of imagination and sparkling temperament. The differences in nature and substance between the naked parts and the loose hair of the figures, the pliable stuffs of the garments, and the metal of the weapons, are brilliantly rendered. The over-all effect is one of power and vigour; at the same time it is decorative and festive, and marked by a spiritualized, sublime sensuousness.

Ch. Picard et P. de la Coste-Messelière, Fouilles de Delphes IV, 2, page 72 ff., plates 7—15. — *P. de la Coste-Messelier,* Au Museée de Delphes (1936), 237 ff. and the same, Bulletin de Correspondance Hellénique 68/69, 1944/45, 5 ff. — *E. Langlotz,* Zur Zeitbestimmung der strengrotfigurigen Vasenmalerei und der gleichzeitigen Plastik, 17 ff. — *Pauly-Wissowa-Kroll,* Realencyclopädie der klassischen Altertumswissenschaft, Supplement 4 (1924), 1252 ff., No. 29 (Pomtow).

52

SEATED SPHINX. Found on the Athenian Acropolis in 1882/83. Parian marble. Height of fragment 1'9½" (0.55 m.). Acropolis Museum, Athens, No. 632.

The sphinx, an imaginary creature with the winged body of a beast of prey and a woman's head, is repeatedly found in conjunction with lions, panthers, griffins, sirens and other fabulous beings in the friezes with which the Greeks decorated their vessels and utensils during the Archaic period. The name sphinx as applied to this particular hybrid creature, and its appearance in the legend of Oedipus, first occurs in the 6th century B.C. The combination of an animal body with a human head is ultimately derived from Ancient Egyptian art, where the type is confined to beings of the male sex.

If the Greeks in the 6th century B.C. consecrated great free sculptures of sphinxes in their sanctuaries and set them up over tombs, they were to them highly demonic beings. They believed that enormous physical and mental forces were at work in these statues. The sitting sphinx that took its place among the motley plethora of 6th-century statues on the Athenian Acropolis must have had a similar significance.

The front legs and the lower part of the body with the hind legs have been lost. The surviving portion of the thin, sinewy body is modelled in spare forms. Two great wings curving in firm arcs like sickles are attached to breast and back and cover one another. Head and neck are turned to the front above the animal's body, which is seen from the side. The large face with the straight, wide mouth and the slanting eyes surmounted by heavy upper lids forms a soft, full oval. The hair surrounds the high forehead in a great arc of individual, sinuous strands and falls behind the ears to the shoulders. It is held together higher up by a broad band, from beneath which it spreads out at the back in a series of uniform pigtails that taper to a point and are modelled like thick strings of beads. Above the band the hair is summarily indicated by a few sculptured waves, and was rendered in detail with paint. On the crown of the head is a round disc with a peg-hole for a trailer of flowers such as sphinxes wore, or a *meniskos,* a metal rod that protected statues from being dirtied by birds.

The breast and back of the figure are painted down to the wings with a scale pattern in red, black and yellow. The same colours have been used to depict the feathers on the wings.

In date the sphinx must come between the Rider (28, 29) and the Kore in chiton and peplos (41–43). It is also the work of an Attic artist. The broad construction and the soft, full shapes of the face are doubtless attributable to the influence of Ionian island art.

H. Payne and G. M. Young, Archaic Marble Sculpture from the Acropolis 10, plates 5—6. — *H. Schrader,* Die archaischen Marmorbildwerke der Akropolis, No. 372, plate 164.

53–57

STANDING YOUTH. Found 1936 at Anavyssus (in Southern Attica). The base with inscription was found 1938. Parian marble. Height 6' (1.94 m.). National Museum, Athens, Inv. 3851.

The figure stands in the posture of the Archaic statues of youths, but in its inner mobility and the tremendous power of its limbs seems to be breaking away from the severity of the old style. The lively modelling of the athletic body, the radiant glance, the splendid coral-like shapes of the hair that falls in a curve over the shoulders, are in concord with the wealth and interplay of shapes exhibited by the interior and exterior contours. The surface is a warm, reddish brown colour. Remains of red paint are visible on the hair, hairband and pupils. The hair on the head above the hairband is only summarily carved and was formerly completed in paint.

The statue originally stood on a three-tiered base, of which only the middle, rectangular tier, and the statue of Parian marble, have come down to us.

It bears in front the distych:

Στῆθι καὶ οἴκτιρον Κροίσου παρὰ σῆμα θανόντος.

hόν' ποτ' ἐνὶ προμάχοις ὤλεσε θοῦρος Ἄρης.

"Stand and mourn by the tomb of dead Kroisos, whom furious Ares snatched away from among the warriors in the front rank."

While the Corinthian youth from Tenea, now at Munich, (ca. 550 B.C.) (34–36) is still fashioned entirely in the style of the Black Figure vases, this Attic memorial figure of Kroisos already belongs, in its greater corporeality and more opulent modelling, to the period of the early Red Figure style. It must have been carved about 520 B.C.

A. Philadelpheus, The Anavyssos Kuros. Annual of the British School at Athens 36, 1935/36, 1 ff., plates 1–5. — G. M. A. Richter, Kouroi, 198 ff., No. 114, plates 89–90, fig. 317–321, plate 132, fig. 461–462. — E. Buschor, Frühgriechische Jünglinge, 106 ff., fig. 124–126. — To the base: G. Ph. Stevens and E. Vanderpool, with a supplementary remark by David M. Robinson, An inscribed Kouros base. Commemorative Studies in honor of Th. Leslie Shear, Hesperia, Supplement 8, 1949, 361 ff. and Bulletin de Correspondance Hellénique 79, 1955, 208 f., fig. 7–8.

58–61

RELIEFS FROM A SQUARE BASE. Pentelic marble. Height 13" (32 cm.), sides 32" (81 cm.) each. National Museum, Athens, No. 3476.

The base was built into an ancient wall in the cemetery in front of the Dipylon at Athens, together with two other rectangular statue-bases. It came to light in 1922. It has a depression in the upper surface for the plinth of the statue that stood on it. The underside rested on a second base. The uncarved side must have stood against a wall. On the front and two sides it bears reliefs depicting scenes from the life of Athenian youth in the late 6th century B.C.

The front face shows four youths in the starting position for various athletic exercises: on the left a runner at the start, on the right a spear-thrower who is resting the fingers of his right hand on the loop and seems to be testing the point or the balance of the spear with his left. In the centre two wrestlers are practising the holds. One of them has seized the other with both hands by the left fore-arm. The latter is defending himself against the pull by exerting a counter-pressure with his right hand against his attacker's shoulder. – On the left-hand face six youths may be seen playing a ball game in teams of three each. The game evidently consisted in one team throwing the ball as far as possible, while the other caught it and threw it as far back as they could, until one side or the other had been driven behind a fixed mark. The player on the left-hand edge of the relief is in the act of throwing the ball. – On the right-hand face of the base (60, 61) two young men are sitting in the middle, their cloaks over their left shoulders and carrying long staves such as were fashionable in Athens at that time. One of them holds a leashed dog, the other a cat on a lead, which they are setting on to one another. Behind them stand two friends, resting negligently and elegantly on their staves, and watching this entertaining and amusing sport with interest.

Of the ancient painting the vermilion ground on the right and left faces of the base is very well preserved. The bodies and cloaks are modelled with splendid vitality and great plastic beauty. The treatment of the muscles and garments and the anecdotal point of the scenes reappear in a very similar form in the mature vases of Phintias and Euthymedes during the last decade of the 6th century B.C.

A. Philadelpheus, Archäologischer Anzeiger 1922, 56 ff. — J. Mosel, Studien zu den beiden archaischen Reliefbasen vom Kerameikos. Rostocker Dissertation, 1935 (Hildesheim 1938).

62–64

THESEUS CARRYING OFF ANTIOPE. From the west pediment of the Temple of Apollo at Eretria. Parian marble. Height 3'7" (1.1 m.). Found in 1900. Museum, Chalkis, No. 4.

Theseus, the Attic hero of legend, has put his left arm round Antiope, the queen of the Amazons, and lifted her off the ground in order to mount his chariot with her. He is naked save for a short cloak over his shoulders. In his right hand he held the horses' reins. The radiant expression on his face seems to mirror delight at his successful feat and the approaching happiness with his beloved. Antiope, who is making no effort to resist abduction, is wearing a short chiton and over it a close-fitting leather cape, as was customary among the Amazons. The forms are rendered with great sculptural power and a highly refined sensuous charm. The hair of the two figures is modelled with particular decorative splendour and beauty. Theseus's is rather short and lies on the head in parallel waves running from the crown; it is rolled up at the nape of the neck and frames the brow and temples with several rows of individual curls. It was surmounted by a wreath made of bronze. Antiope's long hair, rendered in extremely fine individual waves, is parted in the middle, adorned with a diadem and rolled up at the nape of the neck.

The two figures were carved from a single block of marble and attached to the wall of the pediment by a great right-angled dowel at the back. Theseus's right arm was joined on. The group with the team of horses comes from the right half of the pediment (as seen by the spectator). In the centre of the pediment stood Athene in chiton and cloak, armed with the aegis, bearing a great gorgoneion. The upper part of her body without the head has survived (Museum, Chalkis, No. 5, height 2'5"). To her left – corresponding to the group of Theseus and Antiope – we may assume that there was Peirithoos, Theseus's friend and companion, with his team of horses. In addition, both halves of the pediment contained Amazons shooting bows, of which traces remain. One of them, in a kneeling position and bending her bow, must have been carried off from Greece already in antiquity. Her torso was rediscovered in Rome in 1888, in the former Villa Ludovisi, and now stands in the Palazzo dei Conservatori, the Hall of Archaic Sculpture, No. 12 (H. Stuart Jones, The Sculptures of the Palazzo dei Conservatori [1926], Plate 81).

The style of the figures points to a sculptor from the Ionian islands and a date around 510 B.C. It has affinities with the Parian master of the north-east frieze from the Siphnian treasures-house at Delphi (44–51). It is distinguished by its softer, fuller and more sensuously mobile modelling from the harder and more sober manner of the roughly contemporaneous master of the west pediment at Aegina (69–73).

J. *Kuruniotis*, Antike Denkmäler 3 (1914), plates 27—29. — *A. Furtwängler*, Ägina, 321 ff., fig. 259—260. — *E. Langlotz*, Frühgriechische Bildhauerschulen, 157 f. — *E. Buschor*, Frühgriechische Jünglinge, 135 f., fig. 154. — The torso out of the Villa Ludovisi, Rome, is depicted in: *H. Stuart Jones*, The Sculptures of the Palazzo dei Conservatori (1926), plate 81.

65

ATHENE FROM THE OLD TEMPLE OF ATHENE ON THE ATHENIAN ACROPOLIS.

Parian marble. Height of the whole figure 6′7″ (2 m.). The head was found on the Acropolis in 1863, further fragments in the same place in subsequent years. Acropolis Museum, Athens, No. 631.

The Old Temple of Athene between the Parthenon and the Erechtheum was restored by the Peisistratides in about 520 B.C., and furnished with pediment figures of marble in place of the earlier ones of limestone (24, 25). The theme of one of the two pediments, probably the east pediment, was the struggle of the Olympian gods against the giants. The surviving remnants of the pediment figures are insufficient to enable us to form a detailed picture of the composition. The pediment probably contained a total of three two-figure groups together with a fallen giant in each corner. The figures are modelled like free sculpture.

In or near the centre stood Athene in a long chiton and with a cloak over her right shoulder lunging far over to the right (as seen by the spectator). In addition to the head reproduced here, extant fragments include parts of the upper body and the aegis, the left hand, the right foot and shank with the robe and the long, hanging folds of the cloak. Over her outstretched left arm she held the aegis as a weapon in the battle, while with the spear in her raised right hand she struck at a naked fallen giant at whom her downward gaze is directed. Her helmet is encircled by a flat band containing eighteen equidistant holes in which were set bronze rosettes of apotropaeic significance. The crest of the helmet, also of bronze, has been lost, as have the rosettes. The hair frames the clear brow in firm waves. It falls in long curves over the back and is loosened under the ears into thick strands that lie in front of the aegis. The ears are adorned with round discs that used to bear a metal decoration in the centre.

The Peisistratides assigned the new pediment sculptures on the Acropolis to one of the leading sculptors in Athens at that time. The head of Athene in Plate 65 is not seen diagonally from its right side — the view it presented to anyone standing in front of the pediment — but from its left side, which was turned towards the pediment. It is here set against the head of Theseus from the Eretria pediment (64), a later work from the same decade. Both the Ionian-island artist's soft, gentle modelling that seems to bubble up from within, on the one hand, and the Attic sculptor's firmer, more concentrated forms and more intellectually determined and compact style, on the other, are typical products of two closely neighbouring provinces of Greek art in the late 6th century B.C.

H. Payne and *G. M. Young*, Archaic Marble Sculpture from the Acropolis, 52 ff., plate 35, 1—2; 36. — *H. Schrader*, Die Archaischen Marmorbildwerke von der Akropolis, 345 ff., No. 464, plate 185 ff. — *E. Langlotz* and *W. H. Schuchhardt*, Archaische Plastik auf der Akropolis, 61 ff.

66, 67

GIRL IN SLEEVED CHITON AND CLOAK.

Found on the Athenian Acropolis, 1886 (the head) and 1888 (the torso). White to milky grey marble from Chios (?). Height 22.2″ (55.5 cm.). Acropolis Museum, Athens, No. 675.

The flourishing Athens of the time of Peisistratus (560–527) and his sons (527–514/10) attracted a large number of sculptors and vase painters from abroad, especially from the East, whose activities were not without influence on the evolution of Attic art. Several statues by 6th-century insular Ionian and East Greek artists have been found on the Athenian Acropolis, some of them imported into Attica, some produced in Athens itself.

To judge from its material and style, this little statue of a girl came from the island of Chios. It is valuable on account of its particularly well preserved painting. The slim, delicate figure wears a girded sleeved chiton – formerly dark blue, now almost completely green from oxidization – which she is holding aside with her left hand, and a light-coloured cloak over her right shoulder which is pinned together on the right upper arm and sewn together under the arm. On the figure's right side the folds of the cloak, starting from the gather on the upper arm, are rendered by fine wavy lines, in the same way as the thin material of the chiton. Round the throat the chiton has a single-colour border, at the bottom a broad red meander border enclosed in blue (now green). The cloak is studded with a pattern of fine blue spirals and red triangles and has a border containing a pattern of meanders and crosses likewise enclosed between blue (now green) edges.

The outstretched hand held a bowl or a votive offering. The neck is long and rounded, the head strikingly oval, the face with the long, oval chin, wide mouth and slanting almond eyes beneath the wide curve of the eyebrows, is curiously flat. The hair above the brow is rendered in beautiful sinuous waves, and above this in thick strings of beads emerging in rows from beneath the lower edge of a tall diadem. The upper part of the diadem contains seventeen holes for the attachment of a metal ornament and is painted in front with a palmette-lotus ornament on a blue (now green) background. Behind and below the ears five thick pigtails emerge, of which the two at the back end on the shoulders, while the three others fall in front of the shoulders over the fore-arms and along the breast. Large round discs with a red volute pattern on a blue (now green) background decorate the ears. A green and red painted band encircles the neck.

Only the major contours of the back are sculptured. Like the top of the head that protrudes well above the diadem, the rear of the figure is smooth. The details of the hair that hangs far down over the back in a solid mass, and of the folds of the garments at the rear of the figure, must have been painted in.

In comparison with the more solidly constructed Attic statues of girls from the Acropolis with their relatively harder modelling (41–43, 75–77), this figure is softer, more sensuous, and more decorative in the varied treatment of the drapery and hair. The features are more animated, more expressive than those of the contemporaneous Attic korai. This distinguishes the statuette, which some writers have held to be a small-scale copy of a larger Chiotic work, from the more opulent Parian figures, such as the caryatids from the Siphnian treasury at Delphi – which is a few decades older – or the pediment group from Eretria (62–64), which is of about the same date.

In the winged victory from the Acropolis we have a second work

3 East pediment of the so-called Temple of Aphaia on Aegina. Reconstruction. After Furtwängler, *Aegina* (1906)

from the hand of the same master (Acropolis Museum, Athens, No. 693; H. Payne and G. M. Young, *Archaic Marble Sculpture from the Acropolis*, Plates 50, 4 and 120, 3–4; E. Langlotz, *Frühgriechische Bildhauerschulen*, Plate 84, b; H. Schrader, *Die archaischen Marmorbildwerke von der Akropolis*, 118, No. 68, Plate 88).

H. Payne and G. M. Young l. c. 31 and plate 49, 3—5; 50, 1—3. — H. Schrader l. c. 91 ff., No. 43, plate 60 f. and p. 35, group A. — A. E. Raubitschek, Dedications from the Athenian Acropolis (1949), 14 f., No. 9 and page 484 ff.

68

STELE AT THE TOMB OF ARISTION.   Pentelic marble. Height without base 8′ (2.4 m.). Found 1839 near Velanidesa in Attica. National Museum, Athens, No. 29.

The relief shows a warrior in absolute profile clad in a short chiton falling in narrow folds and armoured with breastplate, greaves and helmet. With his raised left hand he calmly holds the vertical lance, whose butt end rests on the ground. The slight inclination of the head intensifies the compactness of the composition. The tall stele was originally crowned at the top with a palmette. Of the rich painting the red in particular has been preserved, especially on the hair of head and beard, on the armour and on the background of the relief. In addition, the armour is decorated with ornamental patterns and with a lion's head incised on the foremost armour plate over the breast, obviously in imitation of bronze armour.

According to the inscription on the base, the stele marks the tomb of Aristion; according to the inscription on the projection on which the figure is standing it is the work of Aristocles. It is one of the finest and best preserved Attic tomb reliefs from the late 6th century B.C. The rich modelling of the surface and the subtlety of all the details have been admired again and again. The closest parallel to the treatment of the drapery-folds is to be found on the mature vases of Euphronios from the period round 510 B.C. Attempts to identify other works by the hand of Aristocles on the basis of their style have so far been unconvincing.

A. Conze, Die attischen Grabreliefs, vol. 1, No. 3, plate 2, 1. — H. Schrader, Aristokles, in: Die Antike 18, 1942, 95 ff., fig. 2—4.

69–73 and 78–83

PEDIMENT SCULPTURES FROM THE SO-CALLED TEMPLE OF APHAIA ON AEGINA. Parian marble. Glyptothek, Munich.

The figures come from a Doric temple on a high mountain falling steeply to the sea on the northern headland of the island of Aegina. The temple has a ground-plan of 95′ by 45′, with six columns on the short sides and twelve on the long. Most of the figures were found in 1811 in the immediate vicinity of the temple. They were acquired in 1813 by the then Crown Prince Louis of Bavaria, restored 1815–1817 by Thorwaldsen at Rome,

and entered the Glyptothek, Munich, in 1828. Subsequent excavations in the sanctuary of Aphaia on Aegina in 1901 brought to light further fragments, which provided important information concerning the arrangement of the individual figures on the pediments. These fragments remained in Greece and are now in the National Museum, Athens.

The remains of three pediments have been discovered – an older east pediment and the west pediment, dating from ca. 510 B.C., and a second east pediment that is some twenty years later in date than the first. The older east pediment, of which only comparatively few relics have been found, must have been damaged soon after completion and replaced by a new pediment in about 490 B.C. In every case the subject is mythical battles of Aeginian heroes before Troy. Athene stood armed in the centre of the pediment, to be thought of as invisible to those fighting.

The west pediment (69–73), which is divided into two almost identical halves, contains thirteen figures in all – six on either side of the central figure of the goddess (69). To right and left of the centre was first of all a warrior lunging at an already staggering opponent. These were followed on either side by a kneeling archer (73) and a warrior leaning forward in the act of thrusting a spear into his fallen adversary (72), finally the corners were occupied by a dying man (70, 71). The main line of movement in the triangular pediment runs from the centre to the corners. The style of the west pediment is characterized by the way in which the delicate figures are arranged almost like surface ornament, and by the studied treatment of the drapery and the artistic coiffures. The plastic shapes are firmly knit and full of inner life.

The later east pediment (78–83) contains eleven figures in all, that is, two less than the west pediment. Apart from the goddess Athene in the centre (78), we need mention only the figure of Hercules in the act of firing a bow – recognizable by the head of the Nemean lion, which he wears on his head like a helmet. Here again the figures on each side of the pediment were arranged in the same order: right and left of the centre a warrior bearing down with sword and spear upon a sinking foe; next on both sides an attacker (79), who is coming to the victim's aid, a kneeling archer (82, 83), and in the corner a fallen warrior (80, 81). In comparison with the figures on the west pediment those on the later east pediment are not only distinguished by their larger proportions, but are also freer in their movements, more naturally spaced, and liberated from the rigidity that characterizes Archaic figures. A more coherent current of life seems to flow through them: they are the visible expression of a new organic conception of the human body and a new approach to monumental sculpture. The four figures each from the west pediment and the later east pediment at Munich here reproduced are:

the rendering of forms. The modelling of the Salamis relief is softer and places greater emphasis on the sensuous values of the body and drapery. The style resembles that of the stele of a girl from the Giustiniani Collection at Berlin (138, 139) and of the Dying Niobid in the Museo delle Terme (172–175), which belong to insular Ionian art. The choice and arrangement of the plant motifs and the mobile growth of the leaves in the ornamental frieze points in the same direction. The sepulchral relief must also be the work of an Ionian island sculptor, who created this masterpiece soon after the completion of the Parthenon sculptures, in about 420 B.C.

A. Conze, Die attischen Grabreliefs, vol. 2, No. 1032, plate 204. — *H. Diepolder*, Die attischen Grabreliefs des 5. und 4. Jahrhunderts v. Chr., 14, plate 6. —*W. Kraiker*, Römische Mitteilungen 51, 1936, 138 ff.

181

BOY MAKING A GIFT. Bronze. Height 8.4" (21 cm.). Louvre, Paris, No. 1843.

Next to Phidias, Polyclitus of Argos is the most important sculptor of the high Classicism of the 5th century B.C. He worked chiefly in bronze, but according to tradition he also created – in the years following 423 B.C. – the great image of Hera of Argos, which was of gold and ivory. What distinguished his work from that of other 5th-century artists was the well calculated relationship of all parts to the whole. His figures possessed a distinct rhythm that was expressed in their inner and outer equilibrium. Polyclitus not only put the rules of his art to the test in statuary, but also set them down in a treatise of his own bearing the title *Canon*, of which fragments have come down to us through indirect sources. He gave a practical demonstration of the theoretically established proportions of the body in a model figure bearing the same name as his treatise. It was regarded by posterity as a norm and standard.

Not one work by Polyclitus has come down to us in the original, yet we are able to form an accurate picture of his major works – such as the Discobolus (discus-carrier), the Doryphorus (spear-carrier), the Diadumenus (victorious athlete fastening the diadem upon his brow) and the Wounded Amazon – from copies made during the period of the Roman Empire. His style is mirrored in various bronze statuettes, of which the Boy Making a Gift in the Louvre is one of the finest. The weight of the body rests on the right leg, the left is free of weight and placed to one side. The relation between the two halves of the torso is shifted to correspond with this pose. The head is tilted to the right, the side of the carrying leg, and looks down at a votive bowl the youth is holding in his hand. The right arm is raised just enough for its outline to correspond to that of the firm supporting leg. The quietly dangling left arm repeats the contour of the left leg that is placed to the side; the left hand held a staff.

The whole body is included within a fine curve that rises from the unweighted leg, and its structure is moulded and balanced down to the last detail. Every movement begins at the middle of the body and radiates outward. This is also the position of the decisive horizontal in the construction of the figure, on which, at a point outside the body, the axes meet that lead through the eyes and hands. The sculptural construction of the body simultaneously makes clear the action that draws the head and the right hand holding the bowl into relation with one another. The statuette epitomizes the harmonious concord of all physical and mental forces in the shape of an athletically formed youth at the height of Greek Classicism.

The hair is finely chiselled. The eyes are inlaid in silver, the nipples in copper.

A. de Ridder, Les Bronzes Antiques du Louvre 1 (1913), No. 183, plate 19. — *A. Furtwängler*, Meisterwerke griechischer Plastik, 492 f., plate 28, 3. — *C. Blümel*, Der Diskosträger Polyklets (90. Berliner Winckelmannsprogramm, 1930), 6 ff., fig. 1. — *E. Langlotz*, Die Darstellung des Menschen in der griechischen Kunst (Bonn 1941), 20 fig. 9.

182

TOMBSTONE RELIEF OF CHAIREDEMOS AND LYCEAS, from Salamis. Marble. Height 6' (1.81 m.), width 3'7" (1.02 m.). Museum, Piraeus.

Greek funerary reliefs of the Archaic period generally bore only one figure, like the stele of Aristion (68), the likeness of the deceased, usually in a high rectangular field. In the early 5th century a new type of relief made its appearance alongside the old and acquired great importance during the succeeding period: the first figure was joined by a second, so that the two faced one another in a mutual relationship. This new type of composition was the precondition for the two-figure groups and family groups comprising several figures seen on Greek sepulchral reliefs of the Classical period.

The tall relief panel closed at the top by a fillet, which was found on Salamis in 1915, differs from other tombstone reliefs of its time by the fact that the two figures do not face each other but are represented as walking in the same direction along a broad common standing-plane. Their names are written on the fillet above their heads. The life-size, athletic figure in ideal nakedness, Chairedemos, carries on his left arm the round shield and in his hand a spear whose ends were painted; his folded cloak hangs over his left shoulder. The upper part of his body is shown almost from the front. Behind him, half hidden by the shield, goes Lyceas, seen more from the side, in a short belted chiton, also with a round shield on his left arm. He is carrying his spear over his shoulder with the right hand.

Whereas on Greek sepulchral reliefs of the 5th and 4th centuries a distinction is made between the dead and the living through the position in which they face one another, the two warriors on this tombstone are represented as belonging to the same sphere by being shown moving in the same direction. It has thus rightly been inferred that the relief on the tombstone must be for two warriors who fell in battle. It also differs from Attic sepulchral reliefs of the late 5th century through the nakedness of one of the warriors. His well built and fully moulded body was obviously modelled on a bronze from the workshop of Polyclitus. It is directly reminiscent of the latter's Doryphorus or Spear-Bearer, which has only survived in Roman copies.

A second sepulchral stele by the master of the funerary relief from Salamis, who must have been a Peloponnesian sculptor or an Attic sculptor under Peloponnesian influence, is extant and now in the Museum at Worcester/Mass. It comes from Megara and depicts a single warrior turned to the right (*American Journal of Archaeology* 41, 1937, 6. Fig. 1).

A. Phourikis, Ephimeris Archaiologiki 1916; 4 ff., plate 2. — *G. Karo*, Archäologischer Anzeiger 1916, 141 ff. — *H. Diepolder*, Die attischen Grabreliefs des 5. und 4. Jahrhunderts v. Chr., 21, plate 16. — *N. Himmelmann-Wildschütz*, Studien zum Ilissosrelief (München 1956) 19 f.

183

SEPULCHRAL RELIEF SHOWING TIMARISTA AND KRITO. White, large-crystalled marble. Height, including the acroterion 6'7" (2 m.), width 3'2"–2'10" (0.95–0.86 m.). Museum, Rhodes, Inv. 13638.

The monument was found in 1931 during the Italian excavations at Kamiros on Rhodes. It must have been carved there at the end of the 5th century B.C. The distance that separates Rhodes from Attica, at that time the centre of Greek funerary sculpture, explains certain differences of form and style that distinguish this memorial from Attic sepulchral reliefs of the same period. The relief panel tapers slightly towards the top, where it is terminated by a projecting arch that curves over the figures like a roof and is crowned in the centre by an acroterion – originally, no doubt, painted with a palmette. The two figures stand on a groundline that slopes down from left to right. Timarista is shown on the right, standing erect and seen almost in front view; her left leg is placed well to the side, her head is turned towards the girl Krito, whom she embraces with her arm; her hand rests on Krito's neck. Timarista is dressed in a fine linen chiton, over which she wears a belted peplos with an overfold and a veil round her head. Krito – in a long chiton and cloak – has stepped towards her with bowed head; her left hand rests on the older woman's shoulder, her right is raised in greeting. This hand of the gentle, vital younger girl forms the focal point of the relief between the two heads.

It is a picture of tender and cordial affection, and at the same time of a last meeting and farewell between two people who differ from one another only in age and height, posture and dress. As to its meaning, there can be little doubt that the right-hand figure represents the deceased. She has been given a heroic aspect by her solemn, upright stance, by the veil, the expressive pose of the left arm and hand that hang down at the edge of the relief, and by a feeling of withdrawal and distance, almost as though she already belonged to the next world. Possibly the figures are those of mother and daughter.

Stylistically the sculptor was dependent upon Attic models. Nevertheless, the manner in which the drapery is rendered – some of it as heavy cloth, some of it as a thin fabric with fine folds – seems to suggest the presence of an insular Ionian or Eastern Greek element.

The girl's hair was roughened to receive paint.

Clara Rhodos 4 (1931), 37 ff., fig. 10—11, plates 1 and 5, 1 (1931), p. 31 ff., fig. 17, plates 4—7. — *K. Lehmann-Hartleben*, Ein griechisches Grabrelief, in: Die Antike 7, 1931, 331 ff., plates 31—33.

184

ATTIC TOMBSTONE. Found during excavations in the Piraeus in 1837. Pentelic marble. Height 4'8" (1.44 m.). National Museum, Athens, No. 716.

The relief, of which a section showing the heads of the two figures is illustrated, is broken diagonally across from right top to left bottom and only about half of it is extant. It had the rectangular shape customary in Attic sepulchral reliefs during the late 5th and early 4th centuries B.C. It was finished off at the top by a shallow pediment that rested directly upon the antae at the sides without any intermediate horizontal member. On the left sat the dead woman, doubtless clad in a long chiton and cloak like the figure of

Hegeso (185), holding in her hands a small box containing her jewellery. Only the head, covered at the back with a cloth like a veil, remains of the upper part of this figure. The long hair is parted in the middle and plaited into a thick pigtail which is wound round the head. Facing her stand two figures looking down at the seated woman with bowed heads: a youthful female figure in chiton and cloak and a handsome, bearded man in a cloak that leaves the chest bare. In his raised left hand he holds a knotted stick. His right hand is stretched out to the seated woman with the palm open to the front in a gesture expressive of deep emotion. The female figure in front of him has thrown one end of her cloak over her left forearm. Her left hand rests on her hip, her right draws the cloak over her right breast with a beautifully gentle movement.

The relief portrays a family group comprising the dead woman and her close relatives – perhaps a mother with her grown-up children, or her son and his wife, or her daughter and her husband. To judge by the relaxed movements and contours of the figures with their beauty of line, the richly curving folds of the drapery and the finely animated faces, the relief must have been carved by an Attic artist at a date not much later than the tombstone of Hegeso, i. e. in the early years of the 4th century B.C. An insular Ionian influence may be seen in the low, superimposed and elongated folds of the softly modelled drapery.

A. Conze, Die attischen Grabreliefs, vol. 1, No. 293, plate 69. — *H. Diepolder*, Die attischen Grabreliefs des 5. und 4. Jahrhunderts v. Chr., 20 f. plate 14.

185

SEPULCHRAL MONUMENT OF HEGESO. Pentelic marble. Height 4'11" (1.49 m.). Width 3'2" (0.95 m.) below, 3' (0.92 m.) above. National Museum, Athens, No. 3624.

The beauty and harmony of this Attic sepulchral monument have been admired ever since its discovery, in 1870, in its old position in the cemetery before the Dipylon at Athens. As is often the case with Greek funerary reliefs of the Classical period, the two figures are depicted within an architectonic frame. The triangular pediment is decorated in the centre and at the sides with upward-pointing acroteria that once bore painted palmettes. On the horizontal transom that carries the pediment, above the seated figure, her name is incribed: Hegeso of Proxenos (wife or daughter).

She is seated in a chair with her legs so stretched out in the large, rectangular field that she fills the space between the two uprights: her back touches the right-hand pillar, the tip of her left foot on the low stool reaches to the left-hand pillar.

Over her long sleeved-chiton she has cast a broad cloak that drapes the lower part of her body and lightly covers her shoulders. One end is drawn under the left arm and falls down from the chair below the left elbow. The wide overlap swells out in close folds over her lap. The loosely waved hair is held in front by three ribbons and taken up at the back under a fine veil. In her hands she held a necklace that was rendered in paint. Hegeso has taken it from a jewellery case held out to her by her maidservant. The girl wears a long, ungirded garment. The calm eyes of the women meet at the mistress's raised right hand that holds the necklace, linking them in the activity which bound them together during Hegeso's lifetime.

The group is wonderfully integrated, held together at the sides by the curving chair-back and by the long fall of the drapery behind the servant-girl, as well as being framed by the verticals and horizontals of the architecture. The broad sweep of the arms is carried across from one figure, via the jewellery box, to the other, joining the two figures into a single unit. Hegeso's right hand, bent upright from the wrist, forms a strongly marked focal point of the whole relief.

The mental attitude expressed by these figures betrays the proximity of the Parthenon frieze, but the carefully planned composition, the emergent tendency of the figures to stand out freely from the background and the 'rich' treatment of the drapery, show that the monument can have been carved only during the last years of the 5th century B.C.

A. Conze, Die attischen Grabreliefs 1, No. 68, plate 30. — *E. Buschor*, Erläuternde Texte zu Bruckmanns Wandbildern alter Plastik (1911), No. 1. — *H. Diepolder*, Die attischen Grabreliefs des 5. u. 4. Jahrhunderts v. Chr., 27 f., pl. 20.

186

VOTIVE RELIEF WITH ECHELOS AND BASILE. Found in the New Phaleron, between Athens and Piraeus, in 1893. Pentelic marble. Width 2'10" (0.88 m.), height 2'5" (0.76 m.). National Museum, Athens, No. 1783.

This relief comes from a broad stele, formerly standing free on a pillar, the opposite side of which also bears a relief. The two rectangular panels are topped by acroteria, the ornaments on which were executed in paint. According to the inscription on the reverse face, the stele was an ex-voto offering to Hermes and the nymphs. This face, not illustrated here, shows two bearded male figures, one of which is characterized as a river god by short bull's horns, and three nymphs. Facing them is a slim, youthful female figure.

On the face shown here a quadriga is galloping up a strip of rising ground. It is driven by a young man dressed only in a short cloak held together at the breast by a clasp and flapping out behind him. He has his left arm round a girl in chiton and cloak who is standing with knees flexed for balance on the moving chariot and leaning back against the youth. With one hand she grasps the raised edge of the chariot front, with the other she holds aside her cloak. The names Echelos and Basile are cut in the fillet above the heads of the two figures. These are a pair of Attic heroes whose significance is roughly that of Hades and Persephone. Echelos abducted Basile and is now bringing her up out of the Underworld into the light again. Hermes is hastening up the slope in front of the quadriga, also identified by an inscription above his head. In his right hand he holds the *kerykeion*, in his raised left hand he seems to have had a torch, which was painted in, with which to light the way out of the darkness for Echelos and the quadriga.

The style of the relief points to an Attic sculptor from the turn of the 5th to the 4th century B.C.

J. N. Svoronos, Das Athener Nationalmuseum 1, 120 ff., No. 1783, plate 28. — *R. Kekulé von Stradonitz*, Echelos und Basile (65. Berliner Winckelmannsprogramm, 1905) 9 ff., plates 2—3. — *H. K. Süsserott*, Griechische Plastik des 4. Jahrhunderts vor Christus (1938), 99 ff.

187—189

RELIEFS FROM THE BALUSTRADE ROUND THE TEMPLE OF ATHENA NIKE ON THE ATHENIAN ACROPOLIS. Pentelic marble. Acropolis Museum, Athens.

On the high, fortified outcrop of rock with a vertical drop on three sides to the south-west of the Athenian Acropolis, outside the propylaea of Mnesikles, stood the sanctuary of victorious Athene (Athena Nike). A small Ionic temple on this eminence facing east, the so-called Nike Pyrgos, was begun by the architect Kallikrates in 448 B.C. but not completed until after the Peace of Nikias in 421 B.C. In the west it extends as far as the extreme edge of the Pyrgos and its southern wall runs parallel with the southern edge of the latter and a few yards away from it. In the north the Pyrgos runs from the western corner of the temple diagonally north-east, where a stairway is cut into it leading from the approach to the citadel to the place of sacrifice in front of the temple.

After Alcibiades's victory over the Peloponnesians in 410/09 B.C. the Nike Pyrgos was furnished, for reasons of safety, with a balustrade of marble panels 3 ft. 6 in. high. These were smooth on the inside and bore reliefs on the outside. On the top of the parapet was a grille of metal rods. In the south, west and north the balustrade was set right on the edge of the cliff. In the north-east there was a short fourth side running along the stairway from the ascent to the citadel as far as the north-east corner of the temple. About a third of the relief panels are extant in the form of fragments that have been found at intervals from 1835 onwards on the Acropolis and its southern slope.

The subject of the frieze is the celebration of a victory. Winged Nikes are erecting trophies and moving in procession with sacrificial bulls from the north and south sides towards the west, the main side of the balustrade, in the centre of which a seated Athene is receiving the two processions. To the right and left of Athene, Nikes are standing decorating a trophy. Further seated Athenes were represented at the western corners of the north and south sides, who, by the twist of their torsos and one arm, carried on the movement of the Nikes approaching from the east and led the procession on towards the victorious Athene on the west face. On the short eastern side the figures moved with the steps of the stairway from the corner towards the shrine. The leading Nike repeats the movement of the stairs and seems to be climbing up to the temple with the visitor.

The whole composition has often been compared to the Parthenon frieze, on which the seated gods in the east receive the procession approaching from both sides. The design of the frieze is the work of a single Attic master. The execution was probably in the hands of six different sculptors. In comparison with the Parthenon frieze the figures are here more markedly detached from the background. Body and drapery have acquired greater independence and are more clearly differentiated from one another in their sculptural treatment. The movements of the individual figures, which achieve an effect of depth without being superimposed one on the other, have a rare beauty and perfection of balance and flow in an unbroken rhythm from one figure to the next. The rich play of the drapery is splendidly decorative.

The illustrations show the four best-preserved figures.

187 above and 188: From the north face of the balustrade (Acropolis Museum No. 11. Height 3'5", width 4'.). Two winged Nikes are leading a bull to the sacrifice. The left-hand figure is pulling back the recalcitrant animal on a rope, planting her left foot firmly against a rock. The right-hand Nike, in front of the bull, was doubtless trying to restrain it with her right hand by grasping its horn.

187 below: Western panels from the south face of the balustrade. (Acropolis Museum No. 1: height 3'1", width 2'5" and No. 2:

height 2'11", width 1'5".) A helmetted Athene in a long chiton is seated on a rock resting her right arm on her upright shield. The cloak she has cast about her lower body is spread over the rock and the edge of the shield. The upper part of her body was covered by the aegis; on the ground beside her the remains of a trophy, which a Nike with raised arms is decorating, are still visible.

189: Right half of a panel from the south face, on which two Nikes were shown beside a trophy. (Acropolis Museum No. 12. Height 3'6", width 1'8".) A Nike taking off her sandals in order to bring the victory offering barefoot. In the movement of untying the sandal her garment has slipped from her right shoulder. The upper part of her body shows through the thin material of the chiton as though naked. Her cloak is carried from the left forearm right round the figure. It falls round the lower part of the body in sweeping folds, which are long and deep, creating broad valleys of shadow from which the ridges stand out in bright light.

The panels with the seated Athene and the Nike in front of her decorating the trophy are the work of the same master as the Nike removing her sandals. He is the most important artist represented on the frieze. Two different sculptors can be distinguished in the panel on the north face showing the Nikes leading the bull to sacrifice. Each of them was responsible for one of the Nikes, which differ from one another in the particular relationship of body to garments, in posture, and in the style of the drapery.

R. Kekulé, Die Reliefs an der Balustrade der Athena Nike (1881). — *R. Heber-dey*, Die Komposition der Reliefs an der Balustrade der Athena Nike, in: Österreichische Jahreshefte 21/22, 1922/24, 1 ff. — *R. Carpenter*, The Sculpture of the Nike Temple Parapet (1929).

190

STANDING BOY. Pentelic marble. Height 33.6" (84 cm.). Museum, Piraeus. Whereas we possess a comparatively large number of statues of youths dating from the 6th century B.C., which stood on graves as effigies of the deceased and as memorials, only a few corresponding sepulchral statues have come down to us from Classical times. In the 5th and 4th centuries B.C., tombstones carved in the round must have diminished in numbers and importance as compared with funerary reliefs. We occasionally come across statuette-sized sepulchral figures of this kind, shown at the top of a tall pedestal, in representations on the white background of ointment vessels for the dead dating from the second half of the 5th century.

The withdrawn, curiously "twilight" attitude of the body and expression of the face with the large eyes under heavy lids and the slightly drawn-down corners of the mouth — as though the boy had turned away from this world to which he had ceased to belong — render this figure reminiscent of those on Attic funerary reliefs and indicate that this is no ordinary votive statue but a sepulchral statue. It is designed to be seen from the front. Very little weight rested on the left leg; the left foot was placed far back and to the side. The movement initiated by the free leg was not, however, imparted with the same vigour to the upper part of the body. The head with the full, rounded lower face rests almost squarely on the rather broad and short neck, turned only slightly to the left. The dangling right arm is stretched forward — the right hand may have held a scraper or a vessel — the left upper arm is drawn back. This gives a certain hesitancy to the rhythm of the figure, which distinguishes the statue from works of the late

5th century B.C. and, together with the boyish, almost childlike conception, the delicate modelling of the body, the soft forms of the face and the rendering of the hair in mobile tufts, suggests a date in the early 4th century B.C.

The spirit and style of the work make it very likely that the sculptor, who was certainly an Attic artist, also produced sepulchral reliefs, which must be recognizable among those that have come down to us.

W. Kraiker, Ein griechisches Knabenbildnis, in: Die Antike 14, 1938, 196 ff., plates 18—20.

191

TOMBSTONE OF DEXILEOS. Found in front of the Dipylon at Athens in 1863. Pentelic marble. Height with the base 5'8" (1.75 m.). Ceramicus Museum, Athens.

The slightly concave front face of the rectangular base, in which the relief was inserted, bears a four-line inscription in the large, clear letters of the early 4th century B.C. It states in brief and simple words that the tombstone was erected for Dexileos of Thorikos, a young warrior who fell at Corinth in 394 B.C. at the age of twenty. He had particularly distinguished himself in the battle along with four other riders.

The square panel, which is only topped by a projecting pediment with acroteria while the sides are unframed, shows a young warrior galloping over his naked adversary — who has fallen to his knees — and thrusting vigorously down at him with his spear. In his left hand he holds the reins. He is wearing a short, belted chiton, a sword-belt diagonally across his chest and a cloak that is held together by a clasp on his right shoulder and that billows out behind him in broad folds. His foe is supporting himself with his left arm, round which is wrapped a small cloak, on his great round shield. He is striving to protect himself from the spear thrust with the sword in his right hand; the sword sheath is visible on is left hip.

The pose of the warrior fallen to his knees with the outstretched right leg and the foreshortened left shank is borrowed from a famous creation of Phidias's day. The profound conception of combat evident in the portrayal of victor and vanquished still bears the signature of the high Classicism of the 5th century B.C. In this respect Dexileos's tombstone has affinities with the equestrian relief in the Villa Albani (177—179). In its pictorial composition, however, in the stress on parallel and intersecting diagonals, in the twist of the bodies out of the background into the relief plane, in the liberation of the figures from the ground and in the emphasis on psychic values it differs appreciably from the art of the Parthenon and proves itself a typical monument of the beginning of the 4th century B.C.

Bridle, reins, spear, the wreath round the rider's head and his adversary's sword-belt were of bronze. The top of the pediment contains a row of six holes at irregular intervals as though for the insertion of metal objects, perhaps rods as a protection against birds or to hang wreaths and fillets on.

A. Conze, Die attischen Grabreliefs, vol. 2, No. 1158, plate 248. — *E. Pfuhl*, Archäologischer Anzeiger 1932, 1 ff.

192, 193

ATTIC TOMBSTONE. Found at Athens. Pentelic marble. Height 3' (0.93 m.). National Museum, Athens, No. 3472.

The inscriptions on the horizontal beam over the figures state that the tombstone was erected for Theano, the wife of Ktesileos of Erythrai. She sits erect on a stool whose strong, straight legs have been turned on a lathe. Her left foot is set on a low foot-rest. She is dressed in a long, thin sleeved-chiton and a cloak draped round the lower part of her body. She has also a cloth over her back, one end of which she holds in a bundle with her left elbow, while she draws the other end, whose corners lie upon her left thigh, forward over her shoulder with a delicate movement of her right hand. Her loose, wavy hair is tied with a broad band, her ear embellished with a large, round disc. Before her stands her husband – a handsome, bearded man in a wide cloak that leaves his chest bare. He has crossed his left leg over his right and is leaning forward supported by a stick placed under his left arm-pit. His hands are clasped in a gesture that may express submission to his fate. His grave eyes rest upon the sitting woman in front of him.

Although this relief is separated by only two or three decades from the tombstone of Hegeso (185) it differs in a number of characteristic features from the older work, which was still directly influenced by the Parthenon sculptures. The close compositional link between the two figures, which the artist stressed in Hegeso's tombstone by means of the box held by both the figures, the movements of the arms and hands and the inclination of the heads towards the centre is no longer present in this relief. The figures are kept apart by the difference in scale and the wide, blank area of background between them. Each has gained more independence. At the same time they possess increased mobility and have been set free from the background, which – like the figures – has acquired greater autonomy. The position of the woman's head, raised and gazing into space, and the twist of her torso away from the side view and towards the front, make her figure seem remote from that of the man standing in front of her.

The slant of the footstool to the picture-plane and the oval formed by the man's arms are devices employed to achieve the new type of spatial effect aimed at in this relief. The relationship between body and drapery likewise differs from that current during the period of Hegeso's tombstone. Althought, in general, the fabric here still follows the forms and movements of the figures, it is more sharply differentiated from the clothed parts of the body and, in the hang of the garments and the play of the folds, is beginning to live a life of its own as decoration.

S. Papaspiridi, Guide du Musée National d'Athènes. Marbres, Bronzes, Vases (1927), 138 f., fig. 22. — H. Diepolder, Die attischen Grabreliefs des 5. und 4. Jahrhunderts v. Chr., 28, plate 22. — J. Dohrn, Jahrbuch des Deutschen Archäologischen Instituts 70, 1955, 62 f., fig. 3.

194

STANDING NAKED GIRL. Found at Beroea in Macedonia. Bronze, hollow cast. Height 10" (25 cm.). Museum antiker Kleinkunst, Munich, Inv. 3669. Purchased from a dealer in 1909.

To depict Aphrodite completely nude did not accord with the idea of the goddess of love held during the 5th or even the early 4th century B.C. Erotic tendencies, which would have been fostered by Aphrodite's nakedness, were still alien to the conception of her nature current at that time. Praxiteles, in his famous Cnidian Aphrodite, was the first to venture upon the step to total nudity. Thus the bronze statuette at Munich, which was made around the turn from the 5th to the 4th century B.C., must be regarded not as an image of the goddess herself, but as a mythological figure, a servant in the cult of Aphrodite, or a hetaera.

The weight of the delicate figure with its beautiful lines rests on the right leg, while the left is unweighted and placed to one side, so that the axes of the body are tilted. The fine curve of movement, which rises from below, is taken up and carried on by the turn of the head and by the lowered eyes. The upper body is slender, the hair bound with a coif. The arms, which are now missing, were cast separately and attached. The figure probably leant against a pillar with the left arm. In the right hand the girl doubtless held a mirror into which she gazed, a pose that harmoniously rounded off the composition.

The poise and unbroken rhythm, the lively modelling and the girl's calm pensiveness, account for the special charm of this precious and much admired statuette. It has recalled works issuing from the school and followers of Polyclitus, and the suggestion has been made that it may have been produced within the sphere of Argivan art.

J. Sieveking, Münchner Jahrbuch für Bildende Kunst 5, 1910, 1 ff. — E. Buschor, Festschrift für P. Hensel (1923), 231. — W. H. Schuchhardt, Die Antike 12, 1936, 84 ff.

195

COUPLE SAYING FAREWELL, from an Attic funeral vase. Found on Salamis. Pentelic marble. Height of the figures, 14.2" (35.5 cm). Glyptothek, Munich, No. 498. Acquired in 1910.

Slender earthenware vessels on a round base, with a long neck and a curved handle, bearing coloured painting on a white ground, were used in Attica during the 5th century B.C. in the cult of the dead. They were called lecythi and their purpose was to contain the oil with which the dead person was anointed. After the final unction the jar was placed in the grave with the dead or set up on top of the tomb. From this developed the custom of copying the earthenware vessels on a larger scale in marble, decorating them with reliefs instead of painted pictures, and erecting them as a monument.

The vase shown here is an Attic funerary lecythus of this type. The lecythus was originally about 4'3" tall. Only the middle part (height 2'5") is extant. Two figures are portrayed on the same standing-plane: a bearded man in a cloak resting on a (painted) staff held under his left arm-pit, and a young woman in a long chiton and cloak with a veil over her head. They are shaking hands. Are they greeting or taking leave of one another? Are they man and wife or father and daughter? Whom does the monument commemorate? We shall find no unequivocal answer to these questions, because the artist of the relief and his age did not intend to characterize the figures in detail or give an exact account of what was happening. They were concerned, rather, to immortalize the close unity of two people. Nevertheless, the figures seem to stand between two worlds and to belong to both at once: they are united in life and death. The young woman with the veil pausing in her walk must be the deceased, who here takes leave of the man, while he gazes at her.

The splendidly rhythmic figure of the woman, the head of the bearded man, and the style of the drapery, recur in a similar form on an inscribed relief dating from 375 B.C. The Munich lecythus must have been fashioned at this period or a little later.

the hair, which is based on Classical models and which, despite its general disorder, exhibits areas where individual tufts of hair are arranged symmetrically or fashioned into rigid ornamental shapes. The bronze dates from the mid-1st century B.C. It may represent a mythological boxer and have been combined with a second figure to form a group.

The rock on which the figure is seated has been restored.

W. Helbig, Antike Denkmäler 1 (1886), plate 4. — W. Helbig, Führer durch die öffentlichen Sammlungen klassischer Altertümer in Rom (3rd edition 1913), vol. 2, No. 1350. — Ph. L. Williams, American Journal of Archaeology 49, 1945, 332 ff. — To artist's mark: R. Carpenter, Memoirs of the American Accademy at Rome 6, 1927, 133 ff.

262, 263

DEATH OF LAOCOÖN AND HIS TWO SONS. White, fine-crystalled marble. Height 8' (2.42 m.). Vatican Collection, Belvedere, Rome, No. 74.

According to Greek legend, Laocoön, a Trojan and a priest of Apollo, married against the god's prohibition and begot two sons. As a punishment he and his sons were killed by two serpents. In the magnificent section of the second book of the *Aeneid* Virgil has clad the Greek material in Roman garb, by giving the Laocoön episode the character of a prodigy, a grandiose augury foreshadowing the downfall of Troy: the terrible fate that overtook these individuals – Laocoön and his sons – would later befall all Trojans.

The Vatican group was found in 1506 in the spacious palace of Nero on the Esquiline. It did not stand there by chance: the incident from Trojan legend was linked with the city of Rome and the Julio-Claudian imperial house through Aeneas, who came to Latium after the destruction of Troy and became the ancestor of the Romans and the Julian family.

In the group the ghastly occurrence is taking place in front of an altar approached by two steps. The elder of the two sons is still unhurt and striving to free himself from the serpent's coils. The eyes of the younger boy, into whose right side the same beast is plunging its fangs, are already glazed. Laocoön is being bitten in the flank by the other serpent, which he is trying to pull away with his left hand. Racked with pain, his abdomen drawn in, his chest mightily raised, his head thrown convulsively back, he opens his mouth in a groan of agony. This group has been much admired for the vividness with which it captures in stone, at the "psychological moment", suffering humanity fighting in vain against disaster ordained from above.

According to ancient tradition, the Laocoön group was the work of three Rhodian sculptors, Agesandrus, Athanodorus and Polydorus. It is a perfect example of the Late Hellenistic group spread out in one plane like a relief and intended to be looked at from one side only, indeed from a single point. In the inward dissolution of its sculptural form, the extension of the bodies and the virtuosity with which it reproduces intense emotion the group represents a late phase of Hellenistic sculpture. Some scholars ascribe it to the mid-1st century B.C., while others place it in the early Augustan period (ca. 30 B.C.).

Laocoön's raised right arm with the serpent has been restored. It was originally bent more acutely at the elbow and touched the back of the head, which materially alters the outline of the whole group. In addition to numerous other details, the right arm of the younger son and the right hand of the elder have also been restored.

W. Amelung, Katalog der Skulpturen des Vatikanischen Museums 2 (1908), 181 ff., No. 74, plate 20. — G. Krahmer, Die einansichtige Gruppe und die spät-hellenistische Kunst, in: Nachrichten der Gesellschaft der Wissenschaften zu Göttingen 1929, No. 1, 1 ff. — H. Kleinknecht, Laokoon, in: Hermes, Zeitschrift für klassische Philologie 79, 1944, 66 ff. — M. Bieber, Laocoon. The Influence of the Group since the Discovery (New York 1942). — G. M. A. Richter, Three Critical Periods in Greek Sculpture (1951), 66 ff.

264

FEMALE HEAD. Found at Satala, near Erivan, Armenia. Bronze. Height 15.2" (38 cm.). The height of the whole figure was about 7'. British Museum, London, No. 266. Purchased from the Castellani Collection in 1873.

Apart from the head, all that remains of the over-life-size statue is the left hand that held a garment. The back of the head is missing. The eyes were inlaid in coloured material. There are two rectangular holes and cavities in the circlet that runs round the head, on the side with the parting, which served for the attachment of a diadem.

The head is slightly tilted towards the left shoulder. The face is modelled in a triangle but creates an impression of roundness because of the small, soft chin and the symmetrical waves of the hair. Fine curls emerge in front of the ears and lie close to the cheeks, longer curls hang down behind the ears and form in falling a curved ornament resembling the meander. Two thin strands have been combed down over the forehead on either side of the parting in the shape of a pair of open tongs. The emphatically severe, straight nose and the shallow curve of the finely drawn eyebrows above the close-set eyes constitute a formal framework whose severity is mitigated by the mouth and eyes. The heavy upper lids give the eyes a thoughtful expression; the small, full-lipped mouth with the sharply defined Venus's bow of the upper lip is slightly open.

The prototype behind this decorative head was an Aphrodite of the 4th century B.C. A late Greek artist has transformed it, with the aid of a carefully thought-out composition and a cool rendering of forms, which may already be called Classicistic, into the ideal of beauty held by his own age. It is hard to imagine that the statue to which the London head belonged was carved before the Augustan epoch.

R. Engelmannn, Ein Bronzekopf des Britischen Museums, in: Archäologische Zeitung 36, 1878, 150 ff., plate 20. — H. B. Walters, Catalogue of the Bronzes in the British Museum No. 266 and the same, Select Bronzes (1915), plate 13.

CHRONOLOGICAL TABLE

776	Beginning of time-reckoning by Olympiads. Coroebus victor at Olympia.
750—650	Homer's great epic poems collected to form the *Iliad* and *Odyssey*.
ca. 750	First Greek colonies established in Southern Italy and Sicily (Cumae 754; Syracuse 735; Taranto 708; Gela 690; Selinus 628).
after 750	Bronze statuette of a horse. State Museum, Berlin, Department of classical Antiquities (Plate 1).
ca. 700	Warrior from the Acropolis. National Museum, Athens (Plate 2).
ca. 660	The oldest monumental stone carvings in Greece.
ca. 640	The Auxerre Statuette. Louvre, Paris (Plate 6).
before 600	Attic statue of a youth in the Metropolitan Museum, New York (Plates 11–13).
594	Solon is Archon at Athens.
ca. 590	West pediment of the Temple of Artemis, Corfu (Plates 14–17).
ca. 570	Calf-bearer from the Acropolis. Acropolis Museum, Athens (Plates 22, 23).
560—527	Peisistratus, Tyrant of Athens. Succeeded by his sons Hippias and Hipparchus.
ca. 550	Funerary statue from Tenea. Glyptothek, Munich (Plates 34–36).
534	First tragedy performed at Athens (Thespis).
ca. 530	Statue of a girl in chiton and peplos from the Acropolis. Acropolis Museum, Athens (Plates 41–43).
before 525	Siphnian treasure-house at Delphi (Plates 44–51).
ca. 520	Funerary statue of Kroisos from Anavyssos. National Museum, Athens (Plates 53–57).
514/10	End of the tyranny at Athens. The Athenians erect a bronze group of the tyrannicides Harmodius and Aristogeiton by Antenor in their market-place in memory of the murder of Hipparchus (514) and the expulsion of Hippias (510), and as a monument to the new democracy.
ca. 510	Funerary stele of Aristion. National Museum, Athens (Plate 68). – West pediment of the so-called Temple of Aphaia, Aegina (Plates 69–73).
509	Kleisthenes promulgates his laws, which are a democratic extension of the Solonic constitution. The proscription of luxury by Kleisthenes brought Attic funerary sculpture to an end until the Parthenon period.
ca. 500	Phidias and Sophocles († 406/05) born.
500—449	Persian Wars (revolt of the Ionian Greeks 500; Battle of Marathon 490; Salamis 480; Plataea 479).
494	Miletus destroyed by the Persians.
before 480	East pediment of the so-called Temple of Aphaia, Aegina (Plates 78–83). – Standing boy from the Acropolis. Acropolis Museum, Athens (Plates 85–87).
480	Destruction of the Athenian Acropolis by the Persians. Carthaginians attack Greek towns in Sicily. Carthaginians defeated at Himera.
477	A new bronze group of the tyrannicides by Kritios and Nesiotes erected in the Athenian market-place to replace the original group by Antenor, which was removed by the Persians.
ca. 470	Terra-cotta group of Zeus and Ganymede at Olympia (Plates 102, 103). – Charioteer at Delphi (Plates 98–101).
472	Performance of *The Persians*, the earliest extant drama of Aeschylus.
469	Socrates born.
ca. 460	Bronze statue of Poseidon from Cape Artemision. National Museum, Athens (Plates 128–131). – The so-called Ludovisi Throne. Museo delle Terme, Rome (Plates 132–135).
458	*Orestes* of Aeschylus.
456	Temple of Zeus at Olympia completed (Plates 105–123). – Aeschylus dies at Gela in Sicily.
448—432	Beginning and completion of the Parthenon (Plates 140–169). – In 438 the image of Athene in gold and ivory made by Phidias was consecrated.
444	The "sophist" Protagoras of Abdera in Athens for the first time ("Man is the measure of all things").
440	*Antigone* of Sophocles.
ca. 440	Statue of a spear-thrower by Polyclitus. Dying Niobid. Museo delle Terme, Rome (Plates 172–175). – The great Eleusinian votive relief. National Museum, Athens (Plates 170, 171).
431—404	Peloponnesian War which ended, after changing fortunes, in the defeat of Athens.
429	Death of Pericles.
ca. 420	Equestrian relief in the Villa Albani (Plates 177–179).
410/400	Sepulchral relief of Hegeso. National Museum, Athens, (Plate 185). – Reliefs of the Nike balustrade. Acropolis Museum, Athens (Plates 189–191).
406/05	Death of Sophocles and Euripides (born ca. 480).
399	Socrates, aged seventy, forced to drink the cup of hemlock.
387	Plato (429–347) founds the Academy at Athens.
ca. 370	Funerary lecythus with leave-taking couple. Glyptothek, Munich (Plate 195). – Early works of Lysippus.
ca. 360	Early works of Scopas and Praxiteles.
353	Death of Mausolus, viceroy of the Persian kings in

Caria. During his lifetime he had his colossal tomb erected at Halicarnassus; after the death of his sister and wife Artemisia (351) the tomb was richly decorated by the sculptors Scopas, Timotheus, Bryaxis and Leochares (Plates 201–207).

ca. 340   Funerary relief from the Ilissus. National Museum, Athens (Plate 218). – Bases of the columns from the later Temple of Artemis at Ephesus. British Museum, London (Plates 214, 215).

338   Philip of Macedon, the father of Alexander the Great, defeats the allied Greeks at the Battle of Chaeronea.

330   Lycurgus has the statues of the three great tragic poets set up in the newly erected Theatre of Dionysus at Athens.

330/20   Funerary relief of Rhamnus. National Museum, Athens (Plate 219). – Hermes of Praxiteles. Museum, Olympia (Plates 220–223).

336—323   Alexander the Great. After his death his successors (the Diadochi) struggle for predominance. Five monarchies develop out of Alexander's empire: Macedonia under the Antigonids, Egypt under the Ptolemeans (capital Alexandria), Syria under the Seleucids, Bithynia (capital Nicomedeia), and Pergamon under the Attalids.

322   Death of Aristotle (born 384), the teacher of Alexander the Great.

ca. 310   The end of Attic funerary reliefs as the result of a law forbidding luxuries issued by Demetrius of Phaleron. Girl's head from Chios. Museum of Fine Arts, Boston (Plates 228, 229).

280   Athenians vote to erect a statue of Demosthenes (384–322) by Polyeuktos in the market-place at Athens.

272   Taranto occupied by the Romans.

270   Death of Epicurus (born 341).

264   Death of Zeno (born 336), founder of the Stoic philosophy.

264—146   Rome's wars with the Carthaginians (Punic Wars), which ended after varying fortunes in the reconquest of Sicily (Syracuse 212) and Southern Italy (Taranto 209) and the destruction of Carthage (146) by the Romans.

241—197   Attalus I, King of Pergamon.

ca. 240   Temple servant, the so-called Girl of Antium. Museo delle Terme, Rome (Plates 232, 233). – Statue of Nikokleia from Cnidus. British Museum, London (Plate 231). – Bearded bronze head from Anticythera. National Museum, Athens (Plates 236, 237).

ca. 210   Sleeping satyr, so-called Barberini Faun, Glyptothek, Munich (Plates 234, 235).

ca. 190   Nike of Samothrace. Louvre, Paris (Plate 248).

ca. 180   Eumenes II (197–159) erects the great altar at Pergamon as a monument to the victory of the Pergamonians over the Gauls (Galatians) (Plates 238–247).

168   Victory of the Romans over Perseus of Macedonia at Pydna. L. Aemilius Paullus brings vast quantities of Greek sculptures in triumph back to Rome.

ca. 160   Bronze statue of a Hellenistic ruler. Museo delle Terme, Rome (Plates 250, 251).

156   Delegation of Greek philosophers at Rome (Diogenes Critolaus, Carneades).

146   The Romans destroy Corinth. Mummius brings countless art treasures from Greece in triumph to Rome. — The kingdoms of the Diadochi fall to the Romans, some by conquest, some by legal testament: Macedonia 148; Pergamon 133; Bithynia 74; Syria 63; Egypt 30.

ca. 120   Statue of Aphrodite of Melos. Louvre, Paris (Plates 254, 255).

ca. 90   Bronze head from Delos. National Museum, Athens (Plate 258).

86   Sulla conquers Athens. The fortifications in the Piraeus are dismantled.

ca. 40   The Laocoön group. Vatican Collections, Rome, Belvedere (Plates 262, 263).

31   Octavian defeats Antony at Actium and becomes emperor – Caesar Octavianus Augustus († A.D. 14).

117—138   Emporer Hadrian. Makes repeated visits to Greece, whose art he admires and fosters. 124/25 he receives the great sacraments at Eleusis.

ca. 160   The Greek travel-writer Pausanias in Greece.

267   Heruli and Goths conquer Athens and plunder shrines throughout Greece.

323—337   Constantine the Great. Christianity is made state religion in the Roman Empire.

393   Last Olympic Games under Theodosius.

410   Rome plundered by Alaric.

476   Romulus Augustulus, last West Roman Emperor.

529   The Academy at Athens closed by an edict of Emperor Justinian.

1204—1456   Greece under the Franks and Venetians.

1456—1821   After the conquest of Constantinople by the Turks (1453), Greece falls into their hands. The Venetians retain fortified trading bases.

1506   The Laocoön group found in Rome (Plate 262, 263).

1764   J. J. Winckelmann's *History of the Art of Antiquity* published.

1766   Lessing's essay *Laocoön, or concerning the Limits of Painting and Poetry, Part I* published.

1786—88   Goethe in Italy.

1802   The Parthenon sculptures brought to London by Lord Elgin.

1811   The pediment sculptures of the so-called Temple of Aphaia on Aegina found [now in the Glyptothek, Munich (Plates 69–73 and 78–83)].

1812   The metopes and frieze of the Temple of Apollo at Phigalia found (now in the British Museum, London).

1821—33   Greek wars of liberation against the Turks, who are forced to evacuate the Athenian Acropolis in 1833 on the insistence of the Great Powers.

1857—58	British excavations at Halicarnassus, Cnidus and Miletus (C. T. Newton).		der P. Kavvadias and G. Kawerau begun in 1882.
1870—74	Terra-cottas found at Tanagra (Boeotia).	1893	*Masterpieces of Greek Sculpture* by Adolf Furt-wängler.
1871—90	Heinrich Schliemann's excavations at Troy, Mycenae, Orchomenus and Tiryns.	since 1896	American excavations at Corinth.
1875—81	First German excavations at Olympia. They have been continued since 1936.	since 1900	British and Italian excavations on Crete (Sir Arthur Evans and others).
since 1876/80	French excavations on Delos and at Delphi.	1903/08	R. M. Rilke's sonnets to Apollo in his *Neue Gedichte* ("Early Apollo" and "Archaic Torso of Apollo").
1878—86	First German excavations at Pergamon, resumed after 1900.	since 1910	German excavations in the Heraeum, Samos.
1885—91	Rediscovery of Archaic sculpture on the Athenian Acropolis through systematic Greek excavations un-	since 1914	German excavations in the Ceramicus, Athens.
		since 1930	American excavations on the Agora, Athens.

LIST OF PUBLISHED WORKS ON GREEK SCULPTURE
SELECTED FOR THEIR BEARING ON THE WORKS OF ART REPRODUCED IN THIS BOOK

GENERAL WORKS, ARRANGED CHRONOLOGICALLY

H. Brunn: Geschichte der griechischen Künstler. Vol. 1: Die Bild-hauer. 2nd edition, Stuttgart 1889.

A. Furtwängler: Meisterwerke griechischer Plastik. Leipzig-Berlin 1893.

G. Lippold: Kopien und Umbildungen griechischer Statuen. Munich 1923.

G. M. A. Richter: The Sculptures and Sculptors of the Greeks. 1st edition, New Haven 1929; 3rd edition 1951.

J. D. Beazley and B. Ashmole: Greek Sculpture and Painting to the End of the Hellenistic Period. Cambridge 1932.

A. J. B. Wace: An Approach to Greek Sculpture. Cambridge 1935.

Ch. Picard: Manuel d'Archéologie Grecque. La sculpture. I–IV. Paris 1935–54.

E. Buschor: Die Plastik der Griechen. Berlin 1936.

F. Gerke: Griechische Plastik in archaischer und klassischer Zeit. Zürich-Berlin 1938.

G. Rodenwaldt? Die Kunst der Antike (Propyläen-Kunstgeschichte, Vol. 3, 3rd edition, Berlin 1938; 4th edition 1944).

L. Curtius: Die antike Kunst II, 1. Die klassische Kunst Griechen-lands (Handbuch der Kunstwissenschaft). Potsdam 1938.

W. Zschietzschmann: Die antike Kunst II, 2. Die hellenistische und römische Kunst (Handbuch der Kunstwissensch.). Potsdam 1939.

W. H. Schuchhardt: Die Kunst der Griechen. Berlin 1940.

E. Buschor: Vom Sinn der griechischen Standbilder. Berlin 1942.

G. Lippold: Die griechische Plastik (Handbuch der Archäologie, 5th instalment). Munich 1950.

R. Bianchi Bandinelli: Storicità dell'Arte Classica. Florence 1950.

G. M. A. Richter: Three Critical Periods in Greek Sculpture. Oxford 1951.

R. Hamann: Geschichte der Kunst von der Vorgeschichte bis zur Spätantike. Munich 1952 (pp. 408–778 on Greek art).

ON ARCHAIC SCULPTURE

F. Matz: Geschichte der griechischen Kunst I. Die geometrische und frühharchaische Form. Frankfurt a. M. 1949.

G. M. A. Richter: Archaic Greek Art. New York 1949.

E. Homann-Wedeking: Die Anfänge der griechischen Großplastik. Berlin 1950.

L. Alscher: Griechische Plastik I. Monumentale Plastik und ihre Vorstufen in der griechischen Frühzeit. Berlin 1954.

G. Karo: Greek Personality in Archaic Sculpture. Cambridge/Mass. 1948.

E. Langlotz: Griechische Bildhauerschulen. Nürnberg 1927.

— Zur Zeitbestimmung der streng rotfigurigen Vasenmalerei und der gleichzeitigen Plastik. Leipzig 1920.

G. M. A. Richter: Kouroi. A Study of the Development of the Greek Kouros from the Late Seventh to the Early Fifth Century B.C. New York 1942.

E. Buschor: Frühgriechische Jünglinge. Munich 1950.

— Altsamische Standbilder. Berlin 1934–35.

R. J. H. Jenkins: Dedalica. A Study of Dorian Plastic in the Se-venth Century B.C. Cambridge 1936.

F. R. Grace: Archaic Sculpture in Boeotia. Cambridge/Mass. 1939.

H. Payne and G. M. Young: Archaic Marble Sculpture from the Acropolis. A Photographic Catalogue. London. 1st edition 1936, 2nd edition 1950.

H. Schrader, E. Langlotz und W. H. Schuchhardt: Die archaischen Marmorbildwerke der Akropolis. Frankfurt a. M. 1939.

E. Langlotz und W. H. Schuchhardt: Archaische Plastik auf der Acropolis. Frankfurt a. M. 1940.

K. Schefold: Griechische Plastik I. Die großen Bildhauer des archai-schen Athen. Basel 1949.

G. M. A. Richter: Archaic Attic Gravestones. Cambridge/Mass. 1944.

ON SCULPTURE OF THE 5th AND 4th CENTURIES B.C.

V. H. Poulsen: Der strenge Stil. Studien zur Geschichte der grie-chischen Plastik 480–450 (Acta Archaeologica 8, 1937, 1 ff.).

E. Buschor und R. Hamann: Die Skulpturen des Zeustempels zu Olympia. Text and Plates. Marburg/Lahn 1924.

A. W. Lawrence: Classical Sculpture. London 1929.

G. von Lücken: Die Entwicklung der Parthenonskulpturen. Augs-burg-Cologne-Vienna 1930.

B. Schweitzer: Prolegomena zur Kunst des Parthenonmeisters I. – Zur Kunst des Parthenon-Meisters II. – Phaidias, der Parthenon-meister (Jahrbuch des Deutschen Archäologischen Instituts 53, 1938, 1 ff.; 54, 1939, 1 ff.; 55, 1940, 170 ff.).

E. Langlotz: Phidiasprobleme. Frankfurt a. M. 1947.

E. Buschor: Phidias, der Mensch. Munich 1948.

K. Süsserott: Griechische Plastik des vierten Jahrhunderts v. Chr. Untersuchungen zur Zeitbestimmung. Frankfurt a. M. 1938.

E. Buschor: Maussolos und Alexander. Munich 1950.

H. Diepolder: Die attischen Grabreliefs des 5. und 4. Jahrhunderts v. Chr. Berlin 1931.

K. F. Johansen: The Attic Grave-Reliefs of the Classical Period. Copenhagen 1951.

HELLENISTIC SCULPTURE

G. Dickins: Hellenistic Sculpture. Oxford 1920.

A. W. Lawrence: Later Greek Sculpture and its Influence on East and West. London 1927.

M. Bieber: The Sculpture of the Hellenistic Age. New York 1955.

G. Krahmer: Stilphasen der hellenistischen Plastik (Römische Mit-teilungen 38/39, 1923/24, 138 ff.).

— Nachahmungen des 5. Jahrhunderts in (Pergamenischen Statuen ibid. 40, 1925, 67 ff.).

— Die einansichtige Gruppe und die späthellenistische Kunst (Nachrichten der Gesellschaft der Wissenschaften in Göttingen 1927, 1 ff.).

— Hellenistische Köpfe (ibid. 1936, 217 ff.).

R. Horn: Stehende weibliche Gewandstatuen in der hellenistischen Plastik. Römische Mitteilungen, Suppl. vol. 2. Munich 1931.

G. Kleiner: Tanagrafiguren. Untersuchungen zur hellenistischen Kunst und Geschichte. 15. Suppl. vol. of Jahrbuch des Deutschen Archäologischen Instituts, 1942.

H. Kähler: Der große Fries von Pergamon. Untersuchungen zur Kunstgeschichte und Geschichte Pergamons. Berlin 1948.